STAGE AUTOMATION

Anton Woodward

**ENTERTAINMENT
TECHNOLOGY PRESS**

Systems Series

This book is dedicated to Sharon, Hannah, Luke and Harry

Cover photo: the Impressario stage automation console designed by the author.

STAGE AUTOMATION

Anton Woodward

Entertainment Technology Press

Stage Automation

© Anton Woodward

First edition published August 2008
by Entertainment Technology Press Ltd
The Studio, High Green, Great Shelford, Cambridge CB22 5EG
Internet: www.etnow.com

ISBN 978 1 904031 56 7

A title within the
Entertainment Technology Press Systems Series
Series editor: John Offord
Photographs by the author unless otherwise stated

CODE / SA01-08/08

PREFACE

The purpose of this book is to explain the stage automation techniques used in modern theatre to achieve some of the spectacular visual effects seen in recent years. This book is targeted at automation operators, production managers, theatre technicians, stage engineering machinery manufacturers and theatre engineering students. It is not intended to be an exhaustive reference work detailing the minute detail of motion control, more an overview of how the various disciplines combine to produce a stage automation system.

The various topics are covered in enough detail to provide an insight into the thought processes that the stage automation engineer has to consider when designing a control system to control stage machinery in a modern theatre. These topics include motor selection, determining the level of control complexity, safety requirements, artistic requirements, electrical standards and a host of other considerations.

Anton Woodward
July 2008

CONTENTS

1 A BRIEF HISTORY

Stage machinery is nothing new. Lifts raised animals to the arena floor of the Coliseum in 1st Century Rome. Contemporary reports suggest one of Shakespeare's Globe theatres had a trap door allowing actors to enter the 'hell' below the stage, while winching machinery lowered an actor from the 'heaven' above the stage.

Revolves, curtains and flown scenery have been moved by hand since before Victorian times; ideas introduced by sailors from ship's rigging systems included elaborate pulleys, ropes and methods of counter-weighting when they moonlighted as stage hands. As technology in society has developed so has the complexity of moving scenery on stage.

The invention of the electric motor did not immediately infiltrate the theatre; there were plenty of luddites in the theatre that did not see the need for new technology even back then! Eventually, of course, the electric motor and hydraulics were used to move stage machinery, both for theatre infrastructure and for production use.

The use of electric motors and to a lesser extent hydraulics meant that control systems were required to power and control these motors. Mostly these control systems were of the simple contactor variety although there were a few elaborate methods devised. Contactors provided simple fixed speed control of motors and hydraulic pumps that were

Shakespeare's Globe Theatre.

quite sufficient for some purposes, but did not lend themselves to precise scenery changes. Therefore, hemp systems and counterweight systems were the preferred method of scenery control. This requires the use of flymen to manually fly pieces of scenery, and has the advantage of direct human contact, enabling fairly precise positioning. In addition, a good flyman can gauge his speed quite well too. However, orchestra elevators, large scenic pieces, heavy tabs and safety curtains did employ motors and hydraulics to varying levels of success.

The control systems used for stage machinery right up to the sixties or seventies was very simple 'contactor technology', which proved to be very robust and some of these old control systems are still in regular use.

The use of contactor technology is often overlooked today in the quest for ever more complex technology, but it is worth remembering that no contactor has ever suffered a software glitch or crashed just before a show.

Telemecanique contactor.

The advent of the personal computer in the early eighties, plus cheap electronics, particularly the dramatic drop in the cost of high power semiconductors, gave rise to a phenomenal increase in the use of automation in manufacturing industry. The technology for stage automation came as a by-product from industrial automation. The cheap supply of motor speed controllers, programmable logic controllers (PLCs), and microprocessor based motion controllers eventually found their way into the theatre too. Early attempts at computer controlled powered flying systems reached varying levels of success and some unfortunate early installations have resulted in a certain amount of reluctance from some quarters in allowing computers into their theatres. However, as with all new technology, it eventually matured, to the extent that modern installations can be designed and built with confidence.

The emergence of Microsoft Windows, as a computer operating system has brought further benefits to stage automation control systems. The use of a familiar interface has enabled advanced motion control functions to be programmed into automation cues with minimal motion control knowledge on the part of the automation operator. This alone has produced some wonderful effects on the stage that would have been prohibitively expensive a few years ago and probably impossible a short time previous to that. The development of lighting desks, in particular, has led to a common realisation of what might be possible with automation and thus many of the terms familiar to a lighting desk operator have found their way into the automation operator's language. For example, the idea of cue sheets, follow-ons and macros are as much a part of an automation operator's desk as they are to a lighting operator.

And so, stage automation has reached a level of maturity, an acceptance that motorised scenery is here to stay and that no self-respecting stage spectacular or modern theatre is complete without it.

12 Stage Automation

2 THE RAISON D'ETRE

The purpose of motorised scenery covers many fields, but perhaps the main reasons are artistic, financial and safety.

Some scenery changes would just be too awful to contemplate if they were carried out with hand flown counterweight flying, such as trucks being hand wound across stage and revolves being pushed by a couple of burly stagehands. Everything would move at slightly different speeds, finish their positions at slightly staggered intervals in not quite the right place, and not in time with the music; in short it would look like the proverbial school play! But, with all the moves synchronised together for a smooth transformation of the acting space, with everything stopping together at the right place on the correct beat of the music and with great lighting, the effect can be stunning.

Or, indeed, it might be, so that the audience have barely noticed that a scene change has taken place because it is almost like a scene change from a film. Either way the artistic benefit is often worth the cost of automation. Consider the lair scenes in *Phantom of the Opera* (pictured). The formation of the lair takes a full 27 seconds, not 26 and not 28 – so that when it is fully formed the audience has been treated to an amazing transformation of the space. In other scene changes, the movement occurs during blackout; with

the briefest dimming of the lighting suddenly the whole stage has been transformed, as if by magic.

The financial reason for employing automation is a straightforward calculation between the investment required to automate a piece of scenery and the cost of employing a stagehand to move it manually every performance. There are obvious risks that the automation may fail in some way – which may ruin a good scene change – and that it could be argued that a stagehand would get it reasonably right every night. But then there is the night when the stagehand does not turn up for work or misses his cue. The cost of an automation operator controlling several pieces of scenery is a very attractive proposition to a large scale musical where the intended run is going to be fairly long; however, it is most probably prohibitively expensive for a small play with a short run.

The other important reason for stage automation is health and safety. Traditional counterweight flying, for example, involves the use of counterweight cradles that have to be hand loaded with weights to balance the flown scenery. The very act of loading these weights into the cradle is a health and safety risk; this is because the flyman is expected to pick up fairly substantial weights off the fly floor and twist his back as he loads them into the cradle.

This practice has already been outlawed in the Netherlands by the imposition of EU laws that are technically already in place in the UK. Germany is likely to follow in due course, and where they go, surely the rest of Europe must eventually follow. The other risks posed by counterweight flying is the task of carefully balancing the load as the flats are lifted off the floor and the weight is transferred to the bar. Runaways do occur, although thankfully rarely, mainly due to the skill and diligence of the flymen. Powered flying is being specified in more and more new buildings and in some older ones too as they get refurbished.

The benefits of a good powered flying system are that fit-ups should be much shorter and the technical rehearsal time should be reduced as the 'deads' and cues are programmed very quickly. The shows themselves should benefit from beautiful scenery changes too!

Other reasons for automating might be the obvious, in that the piece of scenery involved is simply too large and heavy to be moved by hand. Or less obvious, that it has to move continually all through the performance. For example, the sea scenery in the National Theatre's Anything Goes moves for a full two hours, and the windmills in the ENO production of *Don Quixote* are a bit arduous for any stagehand to keep going every night!

3 TRADITIONAL FLYMEN VS FLYING AUTOMATION

An argument that has raged for some time is the relative merits of the traditional flyman against the automation of flying in theatre. There are plenty of well-respected people in theatre at every level who do not like the idea of having computer controlled flying in their theatres, but where have these prejudices come from and what perpetuates the fear?

Flying scenery in theatre has traditionally been performed by the flyman standing on the fly gallery manually pulling a hemp rope attached to counterweight cradle that is balanced with the flown load. Some hemp houses rely solely on the strength and skill of the flyman. When given the cue from stage management he will fly the required piece either in or out, often marked with bits of coloured electrical insulation tape to the required position using only his experience to get the piece to the 'dead' at the correct time.

This method of flying is a very simple yet effective method of changing scenes that has been in use now for a very long time. It has the advantage that a human operator is in direct contact with the load and can instantly detect if there is a problem – perhaps if the flat is snagging on an adjacent bar, he can remedy the situation quickly, or at least report back to stage management and perhaps save the show from being stopped.

The dreaded announcement that the show has stopped 'due to technical difficulties', chills even the most seasoned stage manager. The obvious disadvantage with a human flyman is what happens when there are two or more pieces to be moved or what if it is important that the move is visually perfect.

Despite what most flymen may tell you, even the best of them cannot get the piece to hit the stage nicely at the right moment every time. Flymen also have the added disadvantage in that they can ill, want holidays and occasionally get distracted!

Automation, by contrast, does not have any of these disadvantages. However, if the piece fails to move when the 'Go' button is pressed, the cause for non-movement on demand could be a mechanical problem

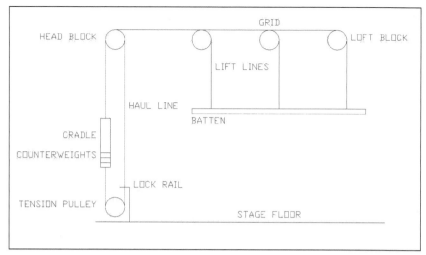

Diagram of traditional counterweight flying system.

that could just as easily have occurred on a counterweight system as a motorised hoist.

A computerised motion control system will sense that the piece is not free to move and cancel the move with a message on screen informing the operator that there is a problem. The fact the computer has put up a fault message often leads to the computer being blamed for the problem – a sure case of shooting the messenger boy! A good automation operator will have 'a feel' for where the problem is just as surely as a good flyman will know where his problem may lie. A good automation system will provide a useful message to the operator to assist him in the rapid remedying of a particular problem.

Other advantages of a powered flying system, often overlooked, is the inherent safety of having an operator watch the piece moving and being able to stop it, either with the 'deadman's handle' or an emergency stop button. The flyman, by contrast, is watching his strips of sticky tape, trying to time his move, with a restricted view of the stage with his back to the moving piece. When multiple pieces have to fly synchronously, then the poor old flyman will be hopelessly outclassed.

These are the arguments that will often be heard in the crew room, however, it will be the money men who decide whether a particular theatre or production will get automation, and whilst they will take on board all that has been explained here, it will be the simple calculation of a flyman's (increasing) wages against the (falling) cost of automation that will prevail in the end.

Powered flying can be achieved in a number of ways, from installing powerful hoists on the grid capable of lifting the full load to fitting small assist motors to existing counterweight cradles so that they only lift the relatively small 'out of balance' load. Counterweight assist can also be achieved hydraulically using 'jigger rams'. This has the added advantage of moving a huge amount of weight quietly and quickly.

Pegasus power flying hoist.

Powerful hoists are often put into a new or refurbished theatre building so that they can be used by any production whereas counterweight assist, either motorised or hydraulic, is usually installed for a specific production. However, there are exceptions to both sets of circumstances, in that counterweight assist can be installed permanently and powerful hoists can be installed for a production. The automation system required for either system is broadly similar, in that the more powerful hoists will have bigger motors and therefore larger drive electronics which will of course be more expensive – hence the attraction of counterweight assist over powerful hoists on cash-strapped productions.

4 STAGE AUTOMATION WITHIN THE GLOBAL INDUSTRIAL AUTOMATION MARKET

The global industrial automation market is worth £70 billion GBP annually; the global stage automation market is estimated at £30 million GBP therefore stage automation represents a tiny fraction of the automation market.

Industrial automation covers mainly factory automation, petrochemical, food and beverage with automotive manufacturing taking the lion's share. With this in mind, it is not surprising that stage automation engineering, as the poor cousin, has to follow the lead set by these global players in major industries, rather than the other way around.

The forces present in the industrial automation market have brought the cost of drive electronics, motion control and programmable controllers down to a level where the relatively small entertainment engineering market can benefit by borrowing the technology. The practitioners of stage automation could just as easily (and some do) earn their living designing and manufacturing control systems for bottling plants and car assembly lines as they could in theatre.

It is the variable speed motor market in particular that has seen a spectacular rise in technology matched by an equally spectacular drop in cost. Twenty years or so ago, variable speed motors were a fairly rare sight in theatre with some very odd-looking contraptions designed to achieve variable speed control. The cyclo-converters at the National Theatre are a good example of an early attempt at variable speed control as well as the huge rheostat that was used to control the DC motors on the revolve at the London Palladium Theatre – made famous by Sunday Night at the London Palladium every Sunday evening on British television in the fifties and sixties.

The major breakthrough for variable speed control came with the miniaturisation of power transistors so that normal industrial three phase motors could be powered from an AC inverter with variable field frequency.

Previously, the speed of a three-phase motor was governed by the field frequency of the mains supply. In the UK this is 50 Hertz (Hz), which meant that a four-pole motor ran at a fixed speed of 1450 revolutions per minute (rpm). The cheap and plentiful supply of power transistors transformed the industrial automation market.

An ABB AC motor inverter.

Other advances in industrial automation technology happening at the same time were the use of programmable logic controllers (PLCs) that replaced relay logic and microprocessor based motion controllers. PLCs enabled banks of relays to be replaced by a controller that could be programmed to perform numerous logic functions. The PLC program is stored in the unit itself on its internal memory and can be re-programmed easily if required or can just be left performing the same routine day in and day out. PLCs are often found in stage machinery control systems such as orchestra elevators, house curtains, revolves, and some simpler power flying systems.

Microprocessor-based motion controllers really opened the way for advanced motion control particularly of powered flying systems and stage automation systems. These motion control boards are able to have speeds, positions, acceleration and deceleration times programmed into them so that movement of scenery and rigging equipment can be finely synchronised or 'choreographed' – and those movements will be replicated performance after performance absolutely perfectly.

Of course, the original purpose of the motion control boards was for use on lathes, milling machines, and other manufacturing machines. Indeed, the Elgo Multiax (pictured right) was one such motion control board that was originally designed for woodworking lathes but found itself on several West End shows during the eighties and nineties including *Beauty and the Beast, Annie, Starlight Express* and *Kiss of the Spider Woman.* As the cost of these industrial automation components came down the market opened up to all sorts of opportunities of which stage automation was only a small part.

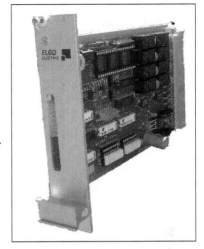

An Elgo Multiax.

Today, the stage automation market relies very heavily on the industrial automation manufacturers; the motor speed controllers and PLCs are still manufactured by large industrial automation companies servicing the petrochemical, food, manufacturing and automotive industries and as such the stage automation companies buy-in this technology as relatively small users. However, the development of custom motion control boards using off-the-shelf microprocessors is an area that a few stage automation suppliers have followed – so that they can offer products to the entertainment industry that are more relevant to powered flying or stage automation than, say, factory automation.

More recent advances in motor technology have produced servomotors, either AC synchronous or asynchronous servomotors, or DC brushless servomotors. These motors provide very dynamic torque characteristics that lend themselves very well to moving pieces of scenery fast. These motors are still relatively expensive when compared to a standard three-phase motor, but as with the drive electronics, these should hopefully come down in cost so that they can be considered for more modest venues and productions in the future.

The future of the industrial automation market is expected to grow steadily, with vast sums of money being spent on research and development. This can only be good news for stage automation as the cost of drive electronics, PLCs, microprocessors and servomotors continues to fall.

22 Stage Automation

5 CONSIDERATIONS WHEN CHOOSING AUTOMATION METHOD

When automation is being considered for a theatrical production the artistic requirement will often dictate the method of motion control. The required speed, noise acceptability, number of deads, weight of the piece to be moved, accuracy of positioning and synchronicity with other moving elements will determine whether motors or hydraulics are used, and the size and type of motor chosen, whether there will be closed-loop position control or whether it will be 'eye-balled' (human operator with a couple of buttons). Once the best way of achieving the artistic effect is determined, and the production can stand the cost of doing it the best way, then the automation engineer has to make it happen. If we take the above points and consider the various alternatives and how they interact with each other, it will be seen that there are many options and combination of options available to the stage automation engineer.

The first consideration is the speed and weight of the piece to be moved. Not surprisingly these two factors have the greatest impact on the basic method of motion and the dimensioning (power) of the motor. Some basic calculations will determine the amount of power that will be required to move the required weight at the required speed. If the piece is being lifted, it will obviously require more power than if it is being tracked across stage; also if the piece has some momentum once moving, consideration has to be given to how it is going to stop. These considerations will decide whether hydraulics or a motor is used and will determine the power of the hydraulic pump and flow rates required or will determine the type and size of the motor.

Hydraulics have the advantage that heavy pieces of scenery can be moved quietly – this is because the pump, which is noisy, can be located some distance from the moving piece. The other big advantage of hydraulics is that if several big pieces have to be moved at different times during the performance then the same hydraulic pump can be used, and the pump, or combination of pumps, only has to be power rated to move the most difficult piece. The various pieces are then all connected to the same hydraulic ring-main with individual valves for the pieces. The downside is that if the pump fails, none of the pieces will be able to move; twin pump packs are therefore usually the norm. Motors are selected when the piece to be moved is either quite small, noise is not such a big consideration, hydraulic hoses would get in the way, the piece requires a greater dynamic response than hydraulics can provide, or if the show has to tour or is in repertory.

Flying systems are mostly motorised; this is usually because of a combination of the above listed factors. Other considerations are that controlling hydraulics accurately is quite difficult, especially as the hydraulic oil heats up and its characteristics change, which causes closed-loop control systems particularly to behave erratically.

Once the basic method, hydraulic or motor, is selected the level of drive complexity has to be determined. At the simplest level the hydraulic method can be

Hydraulic scissor lift.

simply on-off valves (sometimes referred to as bang-bang valves) and the motor method can be fixed speed motors, usually a three-phase motor running direct on line (DOL) at its natural field frequency when powered from the mains electricity supply. The next step up in complexity would be variable speed control; for hydraulic systems this would be by using a proportional hydraulic valve without feedback (open-loop), or in a motor system this would be by using an AC inverter for a three-phase motor or a DC drive for a DC motor. The next step up would be for a closed-loop proportional hydraulic valve or a closed-loop flux vector AC inverter for the hydraulic and motor options respectively. The final step up is the hydraulic servo valve or the servomotor, either AC synchronous or asynchronous servomotor or the DC brushless servomotor. As the level of drive complexity increases, the dynamic response improves, the accuracy of positioning and synchronising improves, and of course the cost increases.

The final part of the jigsaw is the method of control; this can range from a couple of buttons on a pendant to a fully closed-loop computer control system. At the simplest level a couple of buttons could control a bang-bang valve on a hydraulic piece with either a hydraulic knock-off valve or limit

A Lenze Servomotor.

switch determining the 'dead', or the piece could have encoder speed and position feedback back to a computer control system that controls an AC servomotor. At the bottom end of the range, if the piece only has to move between two fixed points at a fixed speed then the bang-bang hydraulic valve or DOL motor with end of travel limit switches may well suffice; the control could be from either a pendant or it could be a simple signal from a computer control system, especially if there are other more complex pieces to be controlled in the same show.

Next up the ladder of complexity may be an AC motor inverter or proportional valve being used just to accelerate and decelerate the piece, but still basically fixed speed between two positions; this would therefore use the simplest control method but the second simplest drive method.

The next level of complexity might be the hydraulic proportional valve or AC motor inverter with closed-loop computer position control; this is about the level of complexity that is most often found for curtain tracks, stage tracks and revolves.

The next level would be closed-loop proportional hydraulic valve or closed-loop flux vector AC inverter with closed-loop computer control of speed and position. The top level would be servo hydraulics or servomotor with closed-loop computer control of speed and position. However, it would be possible, but unlikely, to put open-loop computer control on a DOL motor or put push-button control on a servomotor, so the combinations are quite wide ranging.

So, the automation engineer, in consultation with the set designer and set manufacturing engineers, will have to determine the level of complexity required. To illustrate the point let us take some real examples from various shows over the last few years.

Example one is of a stage lift that was required for *Blue/Orange* at the National Theatre. This required a small area of stage to simply raise and lower a couple of times during the show. Hydraulics was chosen as the main method of motion, since it had to lift several actors silently (the audience would have heard a motorised lift). The lift only had to raise and lower between two fixed positions. Speed and positional accuracy were not great concerns, and therefore a fixed speed hydraulic lift with 'bang-bang' valves controlled from a pendant was the obvious choice. The only other concern on this lift was the safety of the actors as the hole in the stage was filled by the lift descending back to its low position. Safedge was therefore fitted to the outer edge of the moving platform, so that if an obstruction were detected, such as an actor's foot, it would stop the lift descending and not guillotine the unfortunate foot off.

Example two is of six revolving portals for *La Belle*, a ballet by Les Ballets de Monte Carlo. The six portals were arranged in classic portal format – two either side of stage, downstage, mid-stage and upstage. The artistic requirement was that they should have four stopping positions each. The portals were black one side and white the other, and the idea was to have a white box, black box, white portals or black portals.

White representing good and black representing bad, this idea was also used to good effect on *Our House*, the Madness musical. The portals had to move at different speeds, but stop at the same time with reasonable accuracy since if they were not lined up in box format it would be very obvious, with either white stripes in a black box or black stripes in a white box. The other important requirement was that the set had to tour.

The method of motion could only really be motorised, because, on a set that has to tour, hydraulics does get messy when hoses have to be connected and disconnected regularly, it is doubtful that the ballet dancers would have appreciated hydraulic oil on the stage, no matter how well it might have been mopped up. Variable speed was required for two reasons, firstly, the moves had to be done in different times and secondly that large flat portals would wobble horribly if spun and stopped at full speed. Therefore open loop AC motor inverters were specified to control the motors speed. Lastly, a closed-loop computer control system was specified to control the cues because the portals had to do many cues with synchronised movements and with reasonable positional accuracy.

Example three is of a 250kg sheet of glass, travelling at two metres per second across stage. This was the requirement for *Duchess of Malfi* at the National Theatre. The sheet of glass had to position very accurately because images were projected onto it at various positions across stage; also no wobble or judder would be tolerated and the set was in repertory. An AC servomotor with closed-loop computer control was the inevitable method of automation chosen.

6 TOURING, REPERTORY, LONG-RUN CONSIDERATIONS

No matter what the artistic requirement and cost considerations there are factors that will determine the basic design of an automation system that fall outside the criteria of what the control system is actually doing. For example, a control system that has to tour the world will not necessarily be designed in the same way as a control system that is doing the same job but is going to remain in the same theatre for 20 years. These factors are sometimes obvious, like having cables with robust connectors on an automation system that is going to tour, to the not so obvious voltage differences across the world, language problems, spares and technical back-up and automation operators that have their own ideas about maintenance.

An automation system that is going into a venue to stay for a long time, perhaps a permanent flying system, will have different requirements to a system that is in for a specific production or that has to tour. The permanent automation system is likely to be designed and manufactured into steel cased floor-standing or wall-mounted cubicles with all the interconnecting cables neatly fixed to cable tray or laid in cable trunking. The power supply will come from a properly assigned power distribution board and will have the electrical installation inspected by the theatre's insurers, local performance licensing authority, fire brigade and usually a host of other interested parties. There would have been meetings with the theatre management, theatre stage engineering consultants and architects and main contractors; all the technical details will be in a technical file, all the electrical drawings will be controlled documents.

The design of the automation system will have been specified by the theatre consultants on behalf of the theatre, and little choice to the method of motion, drive and control would have been left to the automation engineer. The stage automation engineer would have tendered for the contract, the contract would have been offered to the stage automation specialist who provided the lowest cost (usually). The automation system then provided would be the cheapest that the supplier could get away with whilst still complying with the letter of the contract.

This has inevitably led to some less than satisfactory installations in many theatres that often subsequently require more work and money to bring them up to a reasonable standard. (I could list a few examples here, but wont for fear of getting sued!). The permanent automation system also has many advantages. Firstly, the operator is likely to be on the staff of the theatre rather than the production and so will be very familiar with the automation system and thus get all the benefits of automation. There will probably be several operators who would be properly trained, the control system would be well maintained and therefore reliable, there will most likely be several people in the building at any one time that are capable of using it, either for simply moving pieces during the course of the day or for programming cues and running shows.

An automation system that is going into a theatre for a long running show would have been designed and manufactured to a different set of rules. The first consideration is the length of the fit-up; this will have a major impact on how the control system is designed and manufactured. If 20 or 30 motors with closed-loop computer control have to be up and running in two weeks, then clearly a lot of the work has to be done prior to the fit-up such that the fit-up itself is merely re-connecting motor control cubicles, cables and motors that have already been tested in the workshop as working. This approach to automation means that the cubicles are small enough to be man-handled into a position reasonably adjacent to the motors, the connecting cables are measured and made up with robust connectors prior to the fit-up, and the motors themselves have junction boxes with mating connectors for the motor, brake, position encoder, limit box and any other items that require controlling all made up in advance. The stage automation engineer will have had a fairly free hand in determining the design of the control system using the principles outlined already, with the only proviso that the automation system must be working in time for technical rehearsals and rock solid reliable by first preview. The 'plug and play' method of automation is a well-tried and tested method and only a fool would start trying to wire up cubicles in a theatre during a fit-up. The only exception to this would be for a very simple control system that only requires a day or two of work in the middle of a two-week fit up.

The cable and connector 'plug and play' method is also the method used for touring or repertory. The touring set or repertory set would benefit from very clearly marked connectors, such as colour coded, so that as the set is moved the stagehands can reassemble the system easily. Other considerations for a touring type set is that any faults that the system encounters by having its connectors disconnected or its power downed are either self resetting or extremely obvious to the stage crew. Any automation system that is going to tour or 'rep' has to be built very solidly. The connectors have to be very robust, the cables have to be steel wire armoured and the control pendants, and buttons and indicators have to be of heavy industrial grade.

The internal components within the control cubicles must be able to withstand hours on the road, being bumped off lorries and being left out in the rain.

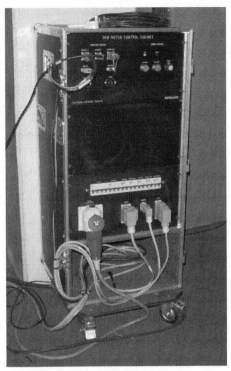

An AVW flightcased control system.

Flight cases are an excellent method of transporting a touring automation system and also make a great touring control system enclosure.

In addition, touring equipment will need to be as unattractive to thieves as possible. Lots of 'Property of someone' labels with indelible ink may make the shiny new laptop less attractive to a thief as well as security chains and password access to the operating system.

Lastly an automation system that is touring overseas may have to work with different voltages in various parts of the world. For instance the UK and Europe is typically 400V three-phase and 200V single phase, however this can vary between about 380V to 440V three-phase or 190V to 250V single phase. A good selection of components, especially power supplies and inverters can ride most of these variations, but touring the USA or Japan and Europe can be trickier. The USA and Japan have 200V three-phase and 110 V single-phase mains supplies. In addition, the mains field frequency in the USA and Japan is 60Hz, except Tokyo which is 50Hz. This can affect the speed of DOL motors and hydraulic pumps. Where an automation system is expected to tour regions with widely varying mains power supplies extra facilities have to be designed in to the control system to cope with these variations. Also the method of voltage selection has to be foolproof. A perfectly serviceable automation system was rendered useless a few years ago on an Elton John world tour, when after Europe the voltage selection was turned down to 110V operation for the USA but not turned back up again when the tour reached Australia!

7 THE PRODUCT-BASED APPROACH

There are quite a few stage automation engineering companies around; and they all approach the design of a stage automation system by one of two methods: either the custom designed system using their own products or by using proprietary equipment from an industrial automation supplier. There are advantages and disadvantages to both methods, however, the 'product-based' approach is gaining popularity.

The advantage of using equipment from an industrial automation manufacturer is that all the research and development would have been done by the manufacturer, albeit for factory automation, so that all the stage automation company has to do is interface his console to suit. The disadvantage of this is that the industrial automation manufacturer would not have designed in anything specifically for the theatre and would be at complete liberty to decide when a particular product becomes obsolete leaving the stage automation company to find another product to control from his console and unable to provide spares in the future.

The advantages of using the product-based approach using the stage automation manufacturers own products are that the stage automation company will be in control of the design and supply of the equipment. Features can be designed in from day one specifically for theatre. The other advantage is that the equipment will not become suddenly obsolete unless it has been planned by the stage automation manufacturer. The disadvantage of this method is that the stage automation manufacturer has to take on the task of research and development of the product. Of course, this could be regarded as an advantage, especially from the customers' perspective, since the stage automation manufacturer can modify and improve his product on advice from his customers.

The product-based approach will ensure that all the stage automation company's installations will be following very similar design principles. This leads to several advantages. The cost of software development will be spread over many projects so that the customer gets facilities that otherwise would have been prohibitively expensive. The spares that the customer has to keep can be kept to a minimum because the stage automation company will be keeping a certain amount of stock in order to keep up with other current projects. Indeed, in an area such as the West End where a stage automation company might have several shows running with their equipment there is likely to be a handy source of spares within a short walking distance. Lead times are kept short because the design is usually a 'cut and paste' process and a decent amount of stock can be held on the shelf in the certain knowledge it will be needed. The stage automation company's engineers will be familiar with the equipment even

A motor control cabinet with proprietary AC inverters and 'product-based' motion controllers.

if they have not seen that particular installation; this will lead to enhanced support both on site and over the telephone. A product-based automation system can be easily expanded, future enhancements to the software can be easily incorporated and automation operators can learn a particular system and take that knowledge to other theatres and shows. In addition, theatre owners and their consultants can visit other theatres where their proposed automation system is already running and see what they are going to get for their money.

8 MOTOR SELECTION

Perhaps the single most important decision in the design process is the correct motor selection. The correct type of motor, power, voltage, brake characteristics, cooling method, over-temperature sensing, coupling and connection method all have to be addressed.

Motor Type

The two main motor types are either DC (Direct Current) or AC (Alternating Current) and then there are further sub-divisions. Listed here are motor types that are now in common use in stage automation; there are other motor types but they are not in common use in theatre today.

DC Motor types:	AC Motor types:
Permanent Magnet,	Single phase,
Shunt wound field,	Three-phase induction,
Series wound field,	Asynchronous servo,
Brushless servo.	Synchronous servo.

Of the motor types listed it would be reasonable to say that only the three phase induction motor and AC servo motor require further study for stage automation purposes. DC motors were once the king of stage automation systems but simpler lower cost AC motors with low cost electronics have all but eliminated them from theatre use now.

Motor Power

After the motor type has been selected then the most important parameter, not surprisingly, is its power rating. The power of a motor is measured in Watts, usually kilowatts (kW) or occasionally Horsepower (HP) (esp. USA). It is preferable to use the SI unit of watts,

A three-phase induction motor.

because the calculations whether electrical or mechanical will be coherent, there are no conversion factors.

For an idea of scale, curtain tracks, floor trucks etc require approximately 1kW of power, small hoists require approximately 4kW, 500kg/1.8m/s hoists require approximately 11kW and orchestra elevators require about 30kW. 1HP is equal to 746 Watts.

It is necessary for the mechanical engineer to calculate the power of the motor required for a particular piece of stage machinery. This calculation will take into account the weight and speed of the payload, whether it is lifting or not and the losses (friction, gearbox efficiency, etc) within the system. It is then incumbent upon the stage automation engineer to ensure that the control system will deliver an adequate amount of power to the motor.

$$\text{Power (W)} = \frac{\text{load kg X G 9.81 X Speed m/S}}{\text{Efficiency}}$$

Motor Voltage

The motor Voltage is usually determined by the power available in the building, which in the UK/Europe is 400-420 Volts AC three-phase or 200-240 Volts AC single phase. However, a single phase supply can be used on a three-phase motor up to about 2.2kW using an AC Inverter (more on inverters later). The general rule of thumb would be to use three-phase if it is available as this keeps the motor current down and hence the conductor size. If only single-phase is available then motor size will most likely be restricted to under 2.2kW.

When preparing automation kit for use in the USA or Japan, then motor voltage becomes slightly more problematic. The mains voltage in USA is 100 volts AC single phase and 220 volts AC three-phase at 60Hz (except in Tokyo). This means that the natural field frequency of the motor is 20% faster.

Motor Current

The motor full load current (FLC) is calculated from the motor power voltage and power factor and is normally given on the side of the motor. This value is the maximum the motor should draw from the control system in normal use. Motor current can go up to 200% of full load current when starting, especially during lifting. However a well designed system will ensure that the FLC is not exceeded for pro-longed periods.

$$\text{FLC} = \text{kW}/1.73 \text{ x Voltage x Power Factor}$$

Power	Three phase Voltages				
kW	220	380	400	415	440
0.37	1.98	1.15	1.09	1.05	0.99
0.55	2.72	1.58	1.5	1.44	1.36
0.75	3.5	2.02	1.92	1.85	1.75
1.1	5.16	2.99	2.84	2.74	2.58
1.5	6.8	3.94	3.74	3.6	3.4
2.2	9.98	5.78	5.48	5.29	4.99
3	12.9	7.5	7.12	6.87	6.48
4	15.7	9.16	8.7	8.39	7.9
5.5	22.6	13.1	12.4	11.9	11.3
7.5	29	16.8	15.9	15.4	14.5
9.3	35.7	20.6	19.6	18.9	17.8
11	42	24.3	23.1	22.3	21
15	54.7	31.7	30.1	29	27.4
18.5	67.5	39.1	37.2	35.8	33.8
22	80	46.3	44	42.4	40
30	105	60.8	57.7	55.6	52.5
37	130	75.2	71.5	68.9	65
45	155	89.6	85.3	82.1	77.5
55	192	111	106	102	96.1
75	253	146	139	134	126
90	311	180	171	165	156

Table of nominal motor currents (Amps).

The values indicated above are those most frequently given for a standard four pole three phase motor.

Motor Speed

All motors will have a nominal top speed usually given in revolutions per minute (rpm). For three-phase motors the nominal motor speed is dependant on the field frequency of the mains.

Synchronous speed in rpm = frequency x 60/no of pole pairs.

In the UK the mains field frequency is 50Hz therefore a four pole motor will have a nominal speed of 1500 rpm. A two pole motor will have a nominal speed of 3000 rpm and a six pole motor will have a nominal speed of 1000 rpm. However three phase motors slip slightly, which means that the rotor is slightly behind the field (stator windings) by about 4% at full torque which means actual rotor speed for a standard three phase motor is 1440 rpm and is usually given as 1450 rpm.

However, stage automation often requires variable speed which means that the field frequency of the mains has to be varied; this is achieved by the use of AC motor inverters.

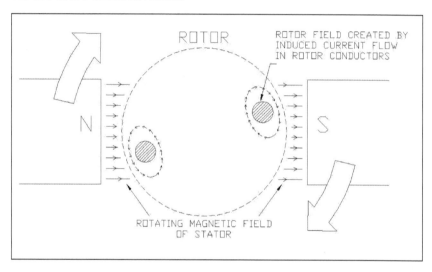

Star or Delta

AC inverters can be fed from either a 200 Volt AC single phase supply or a 400 Volt AC three phase supply. This makes the AC inverter very useful for controlling smaller three phase motors where no three phase supply is available. An inverter that is fed from a single phase supply will only be able to produce a 200 Volt three phase output so the motor will have to be wired for low voltage or 'delta'. An inverter that is fed from a 400 Volt three phase supply will be able to produce 400 Volts so its motor can be wired for high voltage or 'star'. This hold true up to about 7.5kW, where the high voltage is often 600 Volts so the motor has to be wired for low voltage, i.e. delta. It does get a bit confusing, but the motor plate will always indicate the correct configuration.

If 200 Volts is applied to a motor that is expecting 400 Volts then there will be a dramatic loss of torque. If 400 Volts is applied to a motor that is expecting 200 Volts there will be trouble!

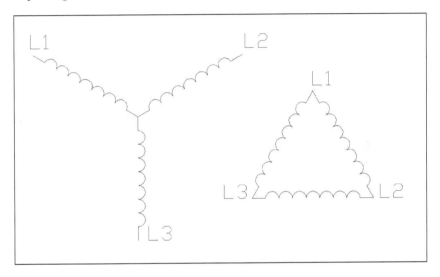

Motor Temperature

The inverter or DOL switchgear will have a means of detecting over current. Over current occurs when the motor is being overloaded, i.e. the full load current (FLC) is being exceeded for a prolonged period. DOL switchgear will have a motor overload device that once tripped will require manually resetting. The overload device will itself remove the three phase supply to the motor and will have contacts so that the control circuit can de-latch any run relays and illuminate any warning indicators. An inverter will normally have a function called I2T where I is current and T is time. The overload trip will occur quicker the more the maximum current is exceeded. However, if an inverter is switched off, or reset, it will forget that it has recently been overloaded. It is for this reason that many motors are fitted with a temperature sensor, normally a PTC (Positive Temperature Co-efficient) switch. A PTC switch will simply become high impedance above a certain fixed temperature and this can be used within the control circuit to prevent operation. This has the advantage that the inverter cannot forget that its motor has been over loaded and over heated.

Three phase motors are often fitted with fans, but theatre motors are often moved slowly such that the fan is having negligible effect. Also it is quite common for the fan to be removed completely so that an encoder can be fitted on the motor shaft. Motor duty times in theatres are much shorter than motors in industry so it would not be often that a theatre motor would get warm so fans and temperature sensors are often missing

Coupling

The output shaft of a motor is usually rotating very fast, typically 1450 rpm at full speed, so motors are normally coupled to gearboxes to reduce the rotating speed to a level that is useful for the application. There are many types of gearboxes (more on gearboxes later), but generally they reduce the motor speed by a ratio that is given on the name plate of the gearbox. A gearbox with a ratio of, say, 40:1, would produce a rotating speed of 36.25 rpm at the output of the gearbox with an input speed of 1450 rpm but with much greater torque.

9 INVERTERS

It is the subject of AC motor inverters that the stage automation engineer has to understand to truly master motor speed control.

As indicated before the speed of a three-phase motor is dependant on the field frequency of its power source. A fixed speed motor could be fed directly from the mains and it would run at full speed all the time. Often this solution is perfectly acceptable for simple hoists, pumps and small mechanisms and therefore direct-on-line (DOL) switchgear is used. It must be remembered however, that DOL starting uses high starting currents and therefore limits the number of starts within a certain period of time; the use of a variable speed AC motor inverter eliminates this problem entirely.

However, it is often the artistic requirement in theatre that dictates the use of a motor speed controller. The hoists, curtain tracks, revolves, etc have to start smoothly accelerating up to a specific speed and decelerate smoothly to a stop. This is achieved by using an AC motor inverter. In simple terms an AC motor inverter is a frequency converter. The incoming mains power which has a fixed frequency (50Hz in the UK) is converted to a variable frequency, usually 0 to 50Hz so that a four-pole motor can have its speed varied from 0 to 1450 rpm. The direction that a three-phase motor rotates depends on the phase rotation of the three phases. Therefore reversal is achieved by reversing any two of the three phases, the inverter also carries out this function. The AC inverter has to be current rated to suit the power of the motor.

There are many manufacturers of AC motor inverters; they are used extensively in manufacturing industry and it is because of this that has driven the price down to a level where they can be used economically in theatre.

All the inverter manufacturers achieve the frequency converter function the same way and so there is little to choose between them on technical grounds but price, availability, ease of

A Eurotherm AC motor inverter.

use and reliability can vary. I have my favourite inverter manufacturers and I am sure that other stage automation engineers have theirs. However, when selecting an inverter the above points, price, availability, ease of use and reliability are of the most relevance. Occasionally, the client will specify the inverters that must be used on a project. This is usually so that they can reduce the amount of spares that they will need to carry if they have several motor control installations; for example air conditioning systems use AC motor inverters for controlling the speed of fans.

An inverter, whether fed from 200 Volts or 400 Volts, will produce a variable voltage and variable frequency, the V/f curve, in response to control signals to vary the speed of the motor. Typically, the control signals will be speed and direction. The speed is usually given as an analogue signal between 0 Volts DC and 10 Volts DC, such that a 5 Volt signal will produce a half speed output. The speed signal can be uni-polar or bi-polar. A uni-polar signal is 0 to +10 Volt, whereas a bi-polar signal is -10 to 0 to +10 Volt. This means that direction is given as well with a bi-polar signal. Where a uni-polar speed reference is used, the direction is normally given with a separate forward and reverse digital input. The inverter will also have other inputs and outputs, typically a brake relay output to control the

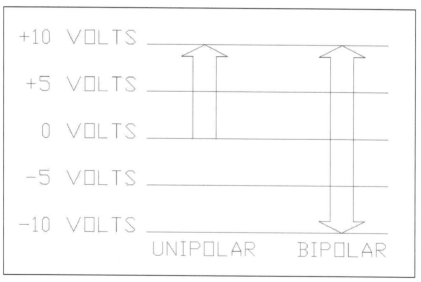

Uni-polar and bi-polar speed reference graph.

motor brake and inputs so that the inverter can be set to fixed (jog) speeds or tripped from external sources.

To truly master stage automation a good understanding of AC motor inverters is an absolute requirement. The AC motor inverter is a variable speed motor controller for AC induction motors. An AC motor's speed is dependent on the mains supply frequency, typically 50Hz or 60Hz, therefore it is this frequency that has to be variable in order for the motor speed to be variable.

This is achieved by first rectifying the incoming mains supply to DC (Direct Current), often referred to as the DC link, and then chopping it up again at a high frequency, and then modulating the three outputs, 120 degree apart, to a pseudo 0 to 50 Hz sine wave approximation.

In addition to the main stages of an inverter, there is some clever electronics going on to ensure that acceleration, deceleration, current sensing, brake switching, motor direction and fault sensing is being handled sensibly.

From the above summary, it is obvious that the inverter has two stages of operation: AC to DC and DC to AC again.

The first stage is called rectification and is quite straightforward. The three incoming phases are connected via filters to the DC Link by diodes.

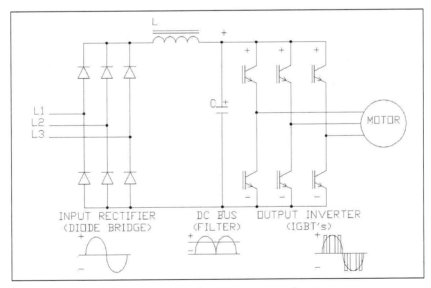

Simplified diagram demonstrating the power stages of an inverter.

The diode only passes current in one direction, like a non-return valve or a one-way street. This enables the positive half of each cycle to be passed to the positive rail and the negative half of each phase to be passed to the negative rail. These half-pulses are then 'smoothed' using large electrolytic capacitors. A useful analogy is to imagine that the capacitor as a water tank being filled with squirts of water at the top and a tap at the bottom of the tank allows the water out as a steady stream; indeed this is often referred to as a 'tank' circuit. The diodes and capacitors are rated to withstand the high voltages and currents involved. A 400VAC three phase input will typically produce a DC link of about 700 Volts DC and a 240VAC single phase input will typically produce a DC link of 375 Volts DC. The fact the input voltage of an inverter is rectified to high voltage DC and smoothed with capacitors means that there will be some current leakage that will often cause a Residual Circuit Breaker (RCD) to trip.

The second stage of an inverter is converting the DC Link back into a variable frequency AC Voltage, and this is not so straightforward. The DC Link needs to be switched at a very high frequency by three pairs of high power transistors to re-produce the three phases. The output therefore is an approximation of a three-phase sine wave. This approximation is achieved by pulse width modulating the switched DC link at the frequency that is required by the motor.

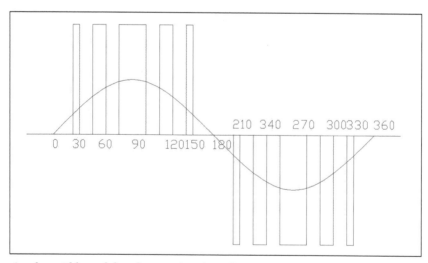

A pulse-width modulated approximation of a sine-wave.

This frequency is determined usually by a 0 to 10 Volt DC analogue signal or sometimes by calling up a jog frequency with a digital input or less usually by a serial command from a computer or PLC. In addition, the output frequency may be adjusted by closed-loop feedback from an encoder to maintain speed holding regardless of load, or may be adjusted by open-loop feedback where the inverter senses the level of slip, often referred to as 'sensorless feedback'. The fact that the output of an inverter is chopped up DC makes the motor output 'noisy' as far as electromagnetic interference is concerned and special consideration has to be given to this. (see EMC section)

Inverter Inputs

The inputs that an inverter requires one way or another are motor direction and speed. At the simplest level this is achieved by a 'forward' digital input, a 'reverse' digital input and a 'speed' analogue input. The analogue speed input is normally 0 to 10 Volts DC; this is referred to as a Uni-Polar signal because the speed signal gives no information regarding direction. An alternative to this, more often used on servo amplifiers, is a Bi-Polar signal. This usually takes the form -10 Volts to 0 Volts to +10 Volts; this therefore gives speed and direction information and the digital input is reduced to just a 'run' signal.

Other inputs commonly found on inverters are Jog inputs; this is where the inverter is programmed to run at a specific speed if the jog input is on. The jog input is often used as a creep speed for stage automation.

Other inputs may include an enable signal, fault reset or parameter set changing.

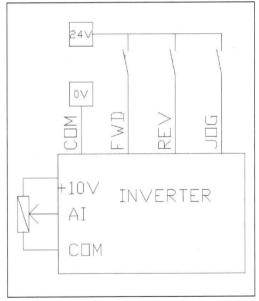

Typical inverter inputs.

Inverter Outputs

Apart from the obvious variable frequency AC output, other outputs from an inverter may include an inverter okay output relay, brake output relay, fault output relay and analogue output.

The inverter okay relay is often the default (and sometimes only) output on an inverter and normally energises when the inverter is switched on with no fault conditions. This relay is often used to indicate to the operator and/or computer control system that all is well.

The inverter fault relay is usually energised when the inverter is switched on but has a fault condition that will prevent it from operating. This is often used to indicate to the operator and/or computer control system that all is not well.

The brake output relay is sometimes a dedicated output but is more usually a normal output that has been configured to operate the brake in a safe manner. The brake output is dealt with more fully on the next page.

The inverter analogue output is often not present but when it is it can be programmed to perform a number of different functions. A non-exhaustive list may include demanded speed, actual speed, actual current and actual torque. This output is not often used, but a specific project may, for example, find a use for displaying motor current to the operator as an indication of running load.

The brake relay from an inverter needs to be handled with extreme care. Often the brake relay is only the brake relay because it has been programmed as such. If the inverter were replaced for instance, the brake relay might suddenly become the inverter okay relay and promptly release the brake as soon as it is powered up. It is therefore very important for the stage automation engineer to ensure that the brake cannot be released until every possible precaution has been implemented to ensure that the inverter has 'got the load' before energising. This is achieved by first ensuring that the inverter is correctly programmed to only release the brake when it can sense that the motor is drawing current, and that there are other relays in the brake release circuit to ensure that the brake is only released during a valid motion command. In addition, particularly for suspended loads, the brake relay will require doubling up for safety redundancy and monitoring to ensure that no brake relays have become 'welded'. It is also very important that should the inverter trip out for any fault condition that the brake output is de-energised immediately.

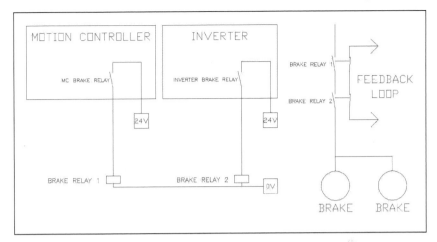

Redundant brake relay switching with monitoring.

Inverter Parameters

When an inverter is first taken out of its box it is generally set up to a default set of parameters. This default setting is often good enough for most applications with relatively little tweaking. However, most inverters have up to 100 or more parameters that can be adjusted to suit specific applications. Typical parameters that can be altered are: the designation of input and output terminals to specific tasks, maximum speed, minimum speed, acceleration, deceleration, current overload, voltage/frequency curve, chopping frequency, torque boost, brake threshold levels and jog frequencies. Most inverters are a variation on a theme and once you can program one inverter then any other manufacturers inverter is not too difficult a task.

Inverters always come with an instruction manual to indicate which parameter does what; the only thing that varies is the ease with which the parameters can be changed, stored and transferred to other inverters. The parameterisation is often performed with three or four buttons and a small LED/LCD screen on the front of the inverter or can be done with the manufacturers' software on a laptop PC connected typically via the serial port. This method is particularly useful if you have a lot of inverters to program in exactly the same way or you need to keep a copy of the inverter parameters for future use. Some inverters have considerably more parameters, whereby quite complex changes can be made to the way the inverter operates, for instance if you wanted to increase the maximum speed of an inverter to 100Hz or more, thereby doubling the motor rated speed, the torque drop-off point may require reducing to flatten off the torque curve. This sort of parameterisation is fairly advanced and will not be considered any further in this text.

The inverter can also perform other functions; it can detect motor overload, i.e. if the motor is drawing excessive current for a period of time it will trip out to protect the motor. The inverter can also detect short circuits and earth faults in its motor output circuit and thus prevent dangerous Voltages being present where it has detected a fault.

Flux Vector

Some AC motor inverters are referred to as closed-loop flux vector inverters. These inverters essentially work in the same way except that there is a feedback device, normally an incremental encoder that provides information on what the motor is doing so that the inverter can control the motor in a much tighter manner. Closed-loop control is almost essential for serious lifting applications such as high-speed hoists and orchestra elevators. Full torque at zero speed is achievable with closed loop flux vector inverters which means that a hoist or an elevator will not 'dip' at the beginning of a lift move and it should be able to come to a complete stop at the end of a move before the brake is applied.

There are also open-loop or sensor-less flux vector inverters without feedback, that rely on a mathematical model to determine control, however these inverters are usually a bit too clever for their own good and in most cases would work better in classic V/f mode, i.e. just like a normal AC motor inverter.

Hoist Runaway

Some hoists are regarded as self-sustaining; this is where the gearbox ratio between the motor and the hoist drum is regarded as high enough that runaway will not occur. Typically a ratio of 40:1 or higher is needed for this to be the case.

A lower ratio gearbox hoist may not start when the brake is let off but this is not a test for self-sustaining, the real test is whether it would come to a stop on its own. If it would not stop then a means of dealing with runaway maybe required.

Regenerative Energy

Some hoists when travelling in the down direction will tend to want to go faster (because of gravity) than the inverter is commanding it to (i.e. runaway). In this instance the motor begins to act as a generator and will create regenerative energy; the inverter can cope with a small amount of regenerative energy but if the regenerative energy is substantial then it has to be dissipated to prevent runaway. There are two basic methods of dealing with 'regen', one is to dissipate it into a regenerative brake resistor and the other is to pump it back into the mains. Pumping it back into the mains is achieved with a regenerative power supply, this is often used with multiple inverters and has the advantage that energy is not wasted or turned into heat. The disadvantage is that if the regenerative power supply fails so do all of the inverters connected to it, this is sometimes regarded as too serious a single point of failure for stage automation so it is not often used in theatre. The more usual method is to dissipate the energy in to a brake resistor using a brake chopper. The energy is given off as heat and this has the advantage that a failure

would be limited to a single axis and can be used on less than perfect mains supplies found in some parts of the world. The brake chopper is sometimes built into the inverter and is sometimes a separate unit. If it is a separate unit, then great care has to be taken in wiring it up because it is connected across the inverter DC link voltage and a reverse polarity connection will make a very loud bang!

The brake resistor will require a thermal switch such that if too much regenerative energy is dissipated into the resistor the inverter can be shut down before the resistor is over-heated and potentially fuse open circuit which in turn could cause a runaway hoist.

Regenerative brake resistor.

Servo

AC Servo drives are very similar to AC motor inverters; indeed some AC motor inverters can control AC servomotors using only parameterisation. The basic rules of AC motor inverters apply to servo drives; it is the motor itself that is different. An AC Brushless servomotor is capable of very high

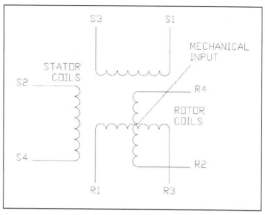

Diagram of a resolver.

speeds, up to 6000rpm, and very high torque giving rapid acceleration and deceleration. A servomotor will nearly always require feedback. Typically a servomotor will be fitted with a resolver for the purposes of feedback. If an encoder signal is required for position control this can often be simulated from the servo drive such that an additional feedback device is not required.

The resolver signal itself is a rotating sine wave that is induced into two windings that are at right angles to each other, thus the sine wave output from the two windings are at 90 degree phasing (Cosine) to each other. The servo drive can use these signals to very accurately determine the position of the rotor and adjust its power output to suit the load.

It is this ability and the very dense magnetic circuit in a servo motor that makes them high performance motors, with a price tag to match.

10 PRACTICAL CONSIDERATIONS IN THE REAL WORLD

The most practical consideration in the real world is, unfortunately, cost. Many a wonderful scheme has been cut back because the budget was not realistic from day one. What was once going to be an all-singing all-dancing variable speed automation system, becomes at a stroke of the accountant's pen, a couple of contactors on a pile wind hoist. However, all is not lost; if the piece of scenery or stage equipment is subjected to a thorough consideration of what it actually has to do on a day-to-day basis then a pragmatic solution can usually be found.

The practical considerations to look at in the real world are:

Load

Positional accuracy

Speed

Number of 'deads'

Travel

Noise

By reducing load, the size of the motor and all its associated control will reduce; the same is true of speed. Reducing the distance travelled by a hoist, for instance, will reduce the size of the drum and hence cost. Other areas that can be looked at are the noise specification, positional accuracy, number of programmable deads - indeed whether programmable deads are even necessary. A specification will often quote a noise specification that even for theatre is quite unnecessary. A figure of 40dBA is sometimes given, that for all intents and purposes is absolute silence. Whereas a hoist with a noise specification of 60dBA could be perfectly acceptable.

11 THE FIT-UP

When a show is installed into a theatre it is called the fit-up. During a fit-up a lot of different trades have to work in the same workspace at the same time. Typically, there will be scenery, lighting, sound, riggers, carpenters, engineers and automation all competing for the same space and time. The production manager will determine a schedule and it is of vital importance that the schedule is workable and that everyone sticks to it.

In order for automation to keep to the agreed schedule, an accurate estimate of the man-hours required to complete the installation has to be worked out. It is then important for the automation team to make sure that they stay on target and if necessary put more people onto the project to ensure that the fit-up is completed successfully and on time.

There are however methods of making life easier for yourself on the fit-up, and the key to that is preparation. When time is tight, it is much easier to go into a fit-up with equipment that is plug and play and has already been set up and tested as far as possible. All the cable lengths should be worked out well in advance, made up, tested and marked at both ends. All motor sizes, brake Voltages, encoder mounting and limit switch positions should be verified with the mechanical contractor. Any potential safety considerations should be discussed with the production manager and other interested parties. Also, if particular help is required from other trades, such as getting riggers to help get automation cabinets to high locations, ensure that it is arranged before the fit-up.

Working Time Directive

Years ago it was quite common to work very silly hours on a fit-up, but thankfully that seems to be a thing of the past. It is important to ensure that the correct numbers of people are on your team and that they get properly rested between shifts. One method to ensure this is to make sure that no-one works more than ten hours a day, have frequent breaks (tea not beer), that they stay near the theatre in a hotel if necessary, and that Sunday is a designated day off.

Working at Height

It is often required to work at height during a fit-up. There are strict laws governing working at height and it is an absolute requirement that these regulations are adhered to without exception. The use of ladders, Tallescopes, scaffolding, etc are all perfectly permissible providing that the correct procedures and safety devices have been implemented.

Consideration

As already stated there are a lot of trades all working together, and it is important that all trades have consideration for each other. Often, a little bit of bargaining, give and take, and respect for what others are trying to achieve will go a long way to a harmonious fit-up.

As an automation engineer, you will be a fairly small cog in a big machine. Whilst it is important to get your bit right, the production as a whole will be judged by the acting, singing, dancing, scenery, lighting and sound. It is therefore important to follow the requirements of the director and designer, work to the production managers schedule, ensure that nobody gets hurt and remember that some of the best automation is barely noticeable by the audience and almost never remarked upon!

12 CUE PLOTTING

A modern stage automation control system will be computer based such that all the moves that the scenery has to perform can be programmed. This is generally done by storing the final demand position, speed, acceleration and deceleration parameters that each motor has to perform. The show will be made up of technical stage management cues that co-ordinate lighting, sound, props, as well as the actors. The stage automation is similarly controlled by cues called from stage management; the automaton operator then actuates the correct cue from his console that will energise the correct motors to move to the scenery to the correct position at the correct speed.

The automation cues will have been determined during the technical rehearsal. Generally this is done by the director giving verbal instructions to the automation operator about where he would like each piece of scenery and how it should move. Some directors are quite clear about what they want and some will try every combination imaginable before settling

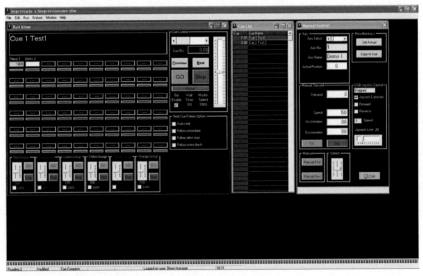

A screen shot from Imressario application software.

on a final position and speed. This is where the flexibility of a computer control system should pay dividends. The automation operator will be able to either in the first case put the position and speed in very quickly and store it or in the second case the operator can show the director several variations that he can choose from.

On other occasions the speed or time it takes to complete a particular move will be determined by music or the time it takes an actor to perform a series of actions. In this case it is beneficial for the automation system to be able to work out the correct speed from the time required and a good automation system will support this function.

It is advantageous if the automation console can be programmed off-line, or on a separate laptop computer, such that cues can be plotted in the rehearsal room. This enables the automation show file to start taking shape before the technical rehearsal. All that then needs to happen is to adjust the positions and speeds in the already created individual cues. Sometimes it is helpful to have an onscreen visual 3D model of the theatre and stage machinery to help plot moves, especially if the moves are particularly complex, such as 3D flying.

At this moment in time all the various stage automation companies have their own methods of inputting the relevant data to construct a cue sheet and their own method of storing that data. This means that the data stored is unlikely to work in another manufacturer's console, unlike say a lighting desk. This has the advantage that the stage automation company can customise their cue sheet structure precisely to their own requirement but has the disadvantage that the cue sheet is not transportable to other manufacturer's consoles. However, it is usually possible to print out the cue sheet data such that if a touring production is going from one theatre with power flying to another with a different power flying system it should be possible to construct a similar cue sheet. In any case the actual target positions are likely to be different anyway because the theatre will have different dimensions. However, it should be possible to move an automation cue file from one console to another from the same manufacturer.

The process of programming the automation cues is probably the best part of an automation operator's duty. The interpretation of the director's vision for moving scenery in a safe, reliable and artistic manner can be quite rewarding.

13 POWER SUPPLIES

The power supply in a theatre can sometimes be a limiting factor to the number of motors that can operate at one time or the weight and speed of scenery to be moved.

Each motor within an automation system will have a power requirement. Therefore the maximum demand on power will be the sum of all the individual motor power requirements.

However, it is unusual to need all the motors at the same time so a level of diversity can usually be applied. In the first instance an idea of what is likely to be required at the same time should be sought and ensure that the power supply is sufficient. In addition, BS7671 states "100% full load current of the largest motor plus 80% full load current of the second largest motor plus 60% full load current of remaining motors".

Once the power requirement has been determined, it is vital to check that it is available in the theatre. If it is not available then some compromises will have to be made or extra power made available. It is not uncommon to find an external power generator outside a theatre when a show is particularly power hungry.

The power supply will often be made available some distance from where the ideal location of the automation rack is. Therefore a consideration is to ensure that the cabling from the power supply to the automation rack is of sufficient cross-dimensional area to handle the maximum current and deal with any potential volt drop. Volt drop is the phenomenon that occurs when current flows in a cable. The longer the cable the greater the electrical resistance to current flow which produces a Voltage potential difference. This Volt drop is reduced by ensuring that the electrical resistance is minimised by using cable of sufficient cross-sectional area. The correct cross-sectional area can be either calculated – there are quite a few websites that will do it automatically – or looked up in tables in the 17th Edition of the IEE Wiring Regulations.

In the UK and Europe the power supply will normally be a nominal 400 Volt three phase AC supply and in USA and Japan the power supply will be a nominal 200 Volt three phase AC supply. The 400 Volt supply in the

UK is actually nearer to 415 Volts, and in other parts of Europe can range from 380 Volts to 440 Volts. This variation in voltage will cause a small variation in current drawn and will need to be taken into consideration when determining the cable requirements.

A neutral conductor will be required when a single phase supply has to be derived from the three phase supply. A single phase supply is simply one of the phases and the neutral. A neutral is not required when the power supply is only supplying a balanced three phase load such as a motor. Most simple chain hoist systems manage without a neutral; this is because the control voltage is usually derived inside the chain hoist from two phases. Since an automation system nearly always requires a single phase supply to power the electronics a neutral is nearly always required. The only exception to this is a cruise ships power supply, where the three phase supply is 'Delta' and therefore does not have a neutral. In this case it is up to the automation manufacturer to derive his control voltage from two phases and transform down to the required Voltage.

The final considerations are to ensure that the power cable is in good condition, well routed and not coiled up in a manner that might give rise to excessive conductor heating produced by eddy currents.

14 REVOLVES

Revolves, turntables, rotating flats and periactoids all have peculiar problems when being automated. That is, there is no beginning and no end of travel, like a scenery bar or curtain track. Sometimes this is not a problem – but on other occasions this can present problems.

Absolute Relativity

Consider a revolve that has encoder feedback for position and speed control. The count from the encoder will hopefully have been scaled to something that is relevant to the real world, perhaps 36000 counts representing 360 degrees. Now consider the following: starting at 0, cue 1 might be one turn clockwise, i.e. 36000, cue 2 might be another turn clockwise, i.e. 72000. Now suppose the director decides to change cue 1 to one turn anti-clockwise, i.e. -36000, cue 2 has all of a sudden become three turns clockwise! This is known as 'absolute' positioning and can be quite a problem for revolves.

One method of overcoming the above problem is to use 'relative' positioning - that is to make each cue a certain number of turns clockwise or anti-clockwise with a final end position. Therefore each cue is simply relative to the last one; this makes life a lot easier if changes are made to the sequence of cues. The disadvantage of relative positioning is that the automation system will be doing a lot of calculations that will ultimately involve some rounding up or down of numbers that may lead to some positional error.

The error will be quite small, however on a revolve that has to position very precisely; perhaps because a track has to line up with it, this may become a significant consideration.

Slip-ring

A revolve or turntable may be required to revolve a number of turns, and on occasion it may be necessary to get power, data or control on board the revolve. In this instance a slip ring will be required. A slip ring is a device that enables an electrical connection through a rotating piece of machinery.

A power or control slip ring will have sprung carbon brushes rotating around stationary rings suitably rated and insulated for the voltage and current required. A data slip ring will have a mercury-wetted mechanism that will allow sensitive data or encoder signals through a rotating joint. It is also possible to fit hydraulic slip rings that will allow a hydraulic connection through a rotating piece of machinery.

Donut Revolves

When a revolve is fitted inside or on top of another revolve it is known as a donut revolve. It may for instance be required to accurately synchronise both revolves together or reverse one revolve such that it appears stationary when on top of another revolve. This is achieved by calculating the relative diameters of the two revolves and ensuring that their relative top speeds are adjusted to the same ratio.

Traction Slip

Revolves are often driven by traction wheels or an endless traction belt or rope. This means that the revolve will be subject to some slip between the motor and the revolve itself. If the encoder is fitted to the back of the motor this will necessarily mean that there will be some positional loss of revolve position. There are two ways to deal with this problem, one method is to fit a datum switch that automatically corrects the encoder count each time it is struck. This will reduce the positional loss to that which occurs between datumming. The other method is to ensure that the encoder is counting directly off the revolve itself regardless of any motor slip that may be occurring.

15 RADIO CONTROL

Occasionally a piece of stage machinery has to travel across stage with no obvious track; this may be because the path is too complex or might be because the path has to be determined interactively. One method of achieving this is by using radio remote control.

Remote control by radio falls into broadly two categories: the first is by using joysticks and operating the machine directly like a radio-controlled car and the other is by using a 'wireless network' similar to a wi-fi network in a house or office. With either method, safety considerations becomes of paramount importance.

Joystick Radio Control

Joystick radio control has been used in theatre successfully for many years. The 'boat' in *Phantom of the Opera* is perhaps the best example. Other projects where I have used this type of radio control include a radio-controlled washing machine that trundled around stage spewing out foam for a Ray Cooney farce and a radio-controlled chaise longue for a ballet in Monte Carlo.

Off-the-shelf model aircraft transmitters and receivers can be used – however, one must ensure that PCM (Pulse Coded Modulation) is used and not PWM (Pulse Width Modulation) type transmitters. Also one must ensure that if the signal is lost or corrupted that the receiver shuts down its output and does not 'coast', which is often the default setting. The receiver is connected to little servos that are normally used for actuating ailerons and rudders but in stage automation are connected to potentiometers that control steering and speed on battery powered DC motor controllers. The risk will always remain that the radio-controlled truck may go awry and

A radio control transmitter.

therefore other risk reducing measures will have to be implemented to ensure that no one is harmed. The most obvious risk is that the truck might go into the orchestra pit; therefore a dip or lip in the stage may be required to ensure that this is impossible. It should also be possible to do an emergency stop on a radio-controlled truck to the correct stopping category as defined by its risk assessment.

This type of radio-control is very manual and may require some skill on the part of the operator, but it is a very useful method of controlling stage machinery where the movement required is complex or interactive.

Wireless Networking

A more recent development in theatre is the ability to connect an automation console to motion controllers wirelessly. This is the same technology as you may have in your house or office whereby an Ethernet network is expanded wirelessly. A method of achieving wireless control is to use proprietary virtual network software so that the connection between the PC controlling

A wireless network router.

the motion controllers is wired but the operator is sitting at a second PC that is mirroring the controlling PC. This has the advantage that the information going over the wireless network is only monitor, keyboard and mouse and not motion control information that may become corrupted. Again it should also be possible to do an emergency stop to the correct stopping category, which may require an independent industrial dual-channel radio control emergency stop system to achieve. Wireless networking can be set up in other ways, such as linking master and slave PLCs over a wireless network or communicating from the console to the motion controllers over a wireless network direct. However, care has to be taken that any corruption of signal does not result in unpredictable behaviour.

This type of radio-control enables pre-programmed cues to be initiated remotely and easy operator intervention as well as interactive operation.

16 CHAIN HOISTS

Chain hoists have been used in the touring entertainment industry for some time, mainly to install quickly fixed trussing in large arena type venues.

However, an area of stage automation that is increasingly popular is the use of industrial chain hoists to move scenery. Several manufacturers produce chain hoist controllers that can provide variable speed control with encoder positioning from a laptop computer. These automation systems are usually a bit simpler than a full-blown stage automation system; however they can be used very effectively in theatre as well as in their more traditional arena environment.

One of the main considerations when using chain hoists in theatre is to ensure that they are correctly specified. Moving scenery, especially over people's heads, requires the use of hoists with fail-safe brakes and fail-safe control systems. There are chain hoist systems that are perfectly safe for rigging a fixed piece of scenery but would not be deemed safe for moving scenery; it is not that uncommon to find theatres using inappropriate chain hoists to move scenery.

The standard to look out for is BGV-C1 (which started life as VBG 70). Unsurprisingly, this is a German standard, from the Institute for Statutory Accident Insurance & Prevention (Berufsgenossenschaft VBG). This is a code of practice that is not enshrined in law – adopting BGV-C1 is entirely voluntary – but its adoption is generally required by insurance companies and has therefore effectively become an industry standard. It is the C1 standard that can be used to move loads over

ASM chain hoist, photo courtesy Charles Haines, Hall Stage.

people; the D8 standard can be used to lift loads during a fit-up with the area underneath cleared of people. A D8 hoist can hold loads over people but not move them; this is is an important distinction.

There are three dominant suppliers of chain hoists in the entertainment industry: Liftket (Chainmaster), Verlinde (Stagemaker) and Columbus McKinnon (Lodestar). Not surprisingly it is the American Columbus McKinnon that is most critical of BGV-C1 and has had to make substantial modifications to its Lodestar to meet the German code. Care should be taken to ensure that any pre-1994 Lodestar hoists intended for flying loads over people have been modified to comply with the standard.

A new standard produced by FEM, the European Materials Handling Federation, called FEM 9.756 is likely in due course to become a European Norm (EN).

17 GEARBOX

Stage automation systems will more often that not be controlling a motor and attached to that motor will be a gearbox. Whilst not strictly a part of the automation system, a wise stage automation engineer will take into consideration the type of gearbox that his controlled motor is driving.

A gearbox uses the principle of mechanical advantage, which is a transmission that provides a torque-speed conversion (commonly known as "gear reduction" or "speed reduction") from a higher speed motor to a slower but more forceful output. The difference in input speed to output speed is usually given as a ratio. For instance a gearbox with a ratio of 40:1, will produce an output speed of 36.25 RPM from a four pole AC induction motor running at a nominal 1450 RPM, however the torque will be forty times greater.

Some of the popular types of gear boxes in use are as follows:
Bevel Gearbox
Helical Gearbox
Right Angle Bevel Gearbox
Spiral Bevel Gearbox
Worm Gearbox

Bevel gearboxes are special speed reducers with their shafts lying perpendicular to each other and therefore used mainly in right-angle applications. The gearbox is a kind of right angle gear and is suitable for a right angle solution with a low ratio. These gearboxes save more energy as compared to worm gears and are available in varying gear ratios

Helical gearboxes are special type of gearboxes finding numerous industrial applications. These gearboxes have teeth that spiral around the gear. These gearboxes are similar to spur gears but have a greater time of contact and are quieter in operation

Gearbox.

Right angle bevel gearboxes have curved and oblique teeth and are used for high speed and high performance industrial machines. The gears are compact and designed for a noise free operation.

Spiral bevel gearboxes are a type of bevel gearbox providing 95-98% efficiency. They are widely used to transmit power between shafts with a right angle orientation to each other. The gearboxes have curved and oblique teeth.

A worm gearbox consists of a shaft with screw thread, also referred as a worm that meshes with a toothed wheel. It changes the direction of the axis of rotary motion.

Helical bevel and worm gear boxes are the ones most encountered in stage automation. Helical bevel are used mostly for fast winches and worm gear boxes are mostly used for slow winches and elevators. A helical bevel gearbox will be quite efficient, losing only about 10% for each spur, therefore on a fast winch the load will be very much at the mercy of gravity and so special consideration to an over-hauling load will be required (see chapter nine for more detail). A worm gear however is much less efficient and will often be capable of holding the load at ratios of about 40:1 and greater. This is often referred to as a self-sustaining gearbox and less consideration to regenerative energy and the effects of gravity are usually required.

It is the potential regenerative characteristics of the gearbox that a stage automation engineer should consider when designing the automation system.

18 NOISE

Noise from stage machinery can be a quite a problem. In an ideal world there would be large pieces of scenery moving with no noise whatsoever. However, in the real world there is motor ring, gearbox whine, brakes clicking, and wire rope dragging on pulleys and other various squeaks and rattles.

There are various ways to deal with different types of noise, so I will examine them here.

Motor Ring

Motors that are controlled from inverters will invariably produce a certain amount of 'ring'. The ring is the chopping frequency of the inverter resonating in the motor windings. It is usually possible to change the chopping frequency from a default 8 kHz (right in the middle of the audible spectrum) to 16 kHz (just above the audible spectrum). There is however a cost associated with doing this, and that is that the switching losses will be higher which may require an inverter of a higher current rating than would otherwise have been the case. The chopping noise can also be exacerbated by having long motor cables; this is because long cables introduce capacitance which tends to 'integrate' the chopping square wave-form. Ideally therefore motor cables are kept as short as possible, and where this is impractical, 'inductance' needs to be introduced to cancel the effects of 'capacitance'. This is done by adding motor chokes at the motor output of the inverter and has the effect of 'rounding-off' the spikes caused by the integrated waveform which in turn reduces the ring.

Gearbox Whine

Gearboxes have a lot of cogs in them all turning and meshing together which creates noise. Obviously the less cogs and less meshing there is will reduce noise. Unfortunately, the gearbox selection will have been mostly determined by load and speed considerations, but if noise were a major consideration then there are some gearboxes that are quieter than others.

For instance a helical-bevel gearbox will be quieter than an equivalent worm gearbox.

Brakes Clicking

A motor brake is an electro-magnetic device that is energised to release the brake and is sprung back to hold the load when de-energised. Usually, both the energisation of a brake and the de-energisation will produce an audible click. Where this is a problem it is possible to purchase special silent brakes; the advantage with these brakes is that often they have been designed specifically for theatre use and comply with all the relevant safety standards, the disadvantage is that they cost more.

Wire Rope

Wire rope can be surprisingly noisy, but there are ways to reduce wire rope noise. One of the main causes of wire rope noise is when the wire rope has to fleet. That is where the rope does not come off its pulley perpendicularly. This can be solved by ensuring that the pulleys are aligned correctly and where movement is required ensure that the pulley is able to adjust itself freely. Another cause of wire rope noise is where the rope leaves a hoist drum. Again the rope is often forced to leave at too great a fleet angle, generally anything more than two degrees is to be avoided.

19 PLCs

PLC stands for programmable logic controller, which is actually a very good description of what a PLC does. In years gone by, the logic of a control system would be determined by the hard wiring of relays, timers, counters and interlocks. Any change to the logic would require a re-wiring of the various relays and timers. Nowadays, all the relay logic can be replaced by a PLC which makes for a lot less wiring and if any changes are required it can be done by a simple bit of programming.

At its simplest level a PLC is a small box of electronics with a few inputs and a few outputs, the state of the outputs, on or off, is determined by the state of the inputs and the logic programmed into it. The complexity of a PLC can be very great where there are many hundreds of inputs and outputs, and analogue inputs and outputs, encoders, temperature sensors, bar code readers, serial ports and programmable touch screens.

PLCs are most often programmed using a special programming language called 'ladder'. This emulates the equivalent hardwired relay logic very closely which in its early days made the programming very easy for electrical engineers. Nowadays, ladder is still a very popular programming method, but other programming methods such as Boolean logic, flow diagrams and statement code are also used. The various PLC manufacturers have their own programming software suites that are functionally quite similar. However, often it is the ease and familiarity of a particular manufacturers programming environment that will determine the choice of PLC used on a particular project rather than the actual hardware.

The inputs of a PLC are normally hardwired to switches, limit switches and the like, the outputs are normally wired to indicator lamps, relays, contactors and in stage automation in particular the forward and reverse inputs of an inverter.

PLCs can also have analogue inputs and outputs which enables variable

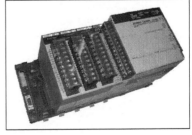

An Omron industrial PLC.

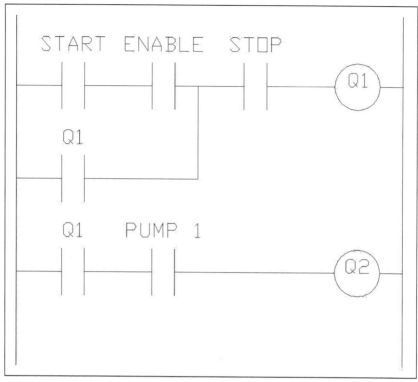

An example of PLC ladder logic.

analogue voltages to be used, for instance as a speed signal. Encoders can also be connected to some PLCs which are useful for controlling position, speed and synchronising of stage machinery.

When choosing a PLC, one has to determine the number and type of inputs and outputs and the approximate size of the program to ensure that a PLC of the correct capability is chosen. Some PLCs are standalone and cannot be expanded and some can be expanded up to a pre-determined number of inputs and outputs, commonly referred to as I/O. A very useful option for controlling a PLC is to use a touchscreen; a touchscreen can have buttons, indicator lamps, text, bar graphs and sliders that can interact seamlessly with the PLC. This enables the man/machine interface to be programmable too, which can make the system very flexible.

Another very useful feature of the more complex PLCs is the ability to distribute I/O over a wide area on a network. This means that numerous limit switches and inverters on, say, the grid can be connected by a two wire network to the master control in, say, the basement. This can reduce the amount and expense of wiring in a building considerably coupled with vast improvements in reliability and flexibility.

PLCs also have serial ports which means they can be hooked up to all manner of external devices such as motion controllers, computers, printers, and LCD display panels and such like.

Some stage automation manufacturers base their automation systems entirely around a particular brand of PLC. This gives them the advantage that all the hardware is available off the shelf from various suppliers and all they have to do is program it for a particular installation. Often the console will use the PLC manufacturer's proprietary touchscreen or will use application software provided by the PLC manufacturer that has been modified or configured for stage automation use. This has the disadvantage that if the PLC manufacturer decides to make a particular piece of hardware or software obsolete the stage automation company may have difficulty supporting the installation beyond a few years. Indeed, this has occurred in one or two high profile projects that have resulted in the automation system having to be replaced much earlier than the client had anticipated.

Some standalone installations such as an orchestra elevator or lighting bridge do not require a full blown automation system and can benefit greatly from a PLC based approach, the proviso being, to ensure that there are enough spares for the anticipated life of the installation.

20 MOTION CONTROL

If the complete understanding of AC motor inverters is an absolute must for the stage automation engineer, then a good understanding of motion control is too. Motion control falls into broadly two types: open-loop and closed-loop. The basic difference between open loop and closed loop is whether or not the motion control system corrects for positional and speed errors whilst controlling the motor. There are many aspects however which remain the same whether open or closed loop.

Most stage automation systems are of the closed-loop type so this is the type that we will look at here.

The drive, motor and mechanical blocks have been dealt with in earlier chapters; the application software, motion controller and feedback device blocks are the subject of this chapter. The same principles can also be applied to hydraulic systems.

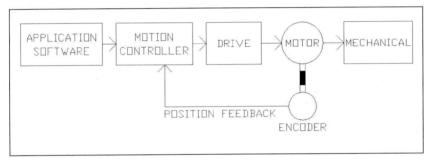

Block diagram of a closed-loop motion control system.

A typical closed-loop motion control system consists of the following components:

Application software – Developers use application software to program desired target positions and motion control profiles.

Motion Controller – The motion controller acts as the brain of the system by taking desired target positions and motion profiles and creating trajectories the motors follow by outputting a signal.

Drive – AC inverter or servo amplifier take the commands from the motion controller and generate the required current to drive the motor.

Motor – Motors are the muscles of the system. Motors convert electrical energy into mechanical energy and produce enough torque to move the motor to the desired target position.

Mechanical Elements – Motors are designed to provide torque to the mechanics via gearboxes such as hoists, lifts, revolves and curtain tracks.

Feedback device or Position Sensor – A position feedback device is vital for closed-loop systems. The feedback device, usually a quadrature encoder, senses the position of the motor and reports the result to the controller. This closes the loop to the motion controller.

Application Software

The various stage automation companies have their own application software, usually loaded on to a computer that may or may not be housed in a console. The application software is typically written using a high-level development software such as Visual Basic, C++ or Delphi. This enables the application software to be written fairly quickly, with a high degree of confidence. An application written in one of these languages

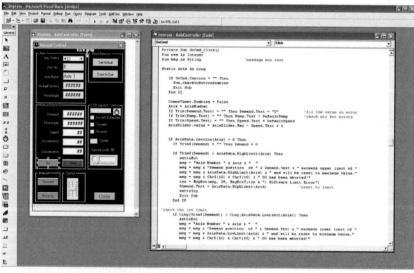

Application software being written in Visual Basic.

would operate within the Microsoft Windows operating system. Some stage automation companies write their application software using other high-level development software to operate in other operating systems such as UNIX or Linux.

Whichever operating system is used and whichever development tool is used, the end result is the application software. The application software is the operator's software for programming and running the cues, setting up the motion controllers, file storage and faultfinding. The software should be as easy as possible for the operator to program and run his cues whilst at the same time giving him the ability to program complex motion profiles. In addition the application software should be able to access the motion controllers so that they can be configured and troubleshot easily and the various motion control parameters edited, stored and loaded readily.

Motion Controller

The motion controller calculates the trajectories for each commanded move. This task is often done on the motion controller to prevent interference from the host computer. The motion controller uses the trajectories it calculates to determine the proper command to send to the motor drive to cause motion.

The motion controller also closes the control loop. Because closing the control loop requires a high level of determinism, it is also typically done on the motion controller. Along with closing

An Impressario motion controller.

the control loop, the motion controller also provides supervisory control by monitoring limits and emergency stops to ensure safe operation.

Calculating the Trajectory

The motion trajectory describes the profile of the control or command signal output by the motion controller board to the drive. This results in a motor/motion action that follows the described profile. A typical motion controller calculates the segments of a motion profile trajectory based on programmed parameter values. The motion controller uses the desired target position, maximum target velocity, and acceleration values to determine how much time is spent in acceleration, constant velocity and deceleration. In the acceleration segment of a typical trapezoidal profile, motion begins from a stopped position, or from a previously in-process move, and follows a prescribed acceleration ramp until the speed reaches the target velocity for the move. Motion continues at the target velocity for a prescribed period until the controller begins the deceleration segment and slows the motion to a stop at the desired target position.

If a move is short enough that the deceleration start point occurs before acceleration has completed, the profile will appear triangular instead of trapezoidal and the actual velocity attained may fall short of the desired target velocity.

An enhancement to the basic trapezoidal profile is S-curve acceleration/ deceleration, where the acceleration and deceleration ramps are modified into a non-linear, curved profile. An S-curve profile allows for fine control over the shape of these ramps and is useful for tailoring the performance of a motion trajectory based on the inertial, frictional forces, motor dynamics and other mechanical limitations of motion systems.

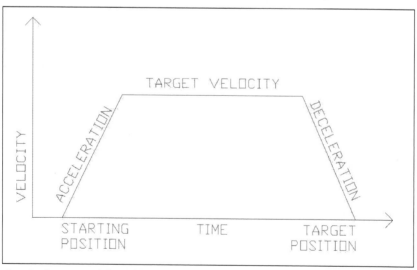

A typical trapezoidal profile.

Feedback Devices

Feedback devices are designed to help the motion controller know where the motor is. The most common position feedback device is the quadrature encoder. A quadrature encoder gives position feedback relative to where it starts. Most motion controllers are designed to work with these types of encoders. Other feedback devices include potentiometers, which give analogue position feedback; tachometers, which provide velocity feedback; absolute encoders, for absolute position measurements; and resolvers, which also give absolute position measurements.

Incremental encoders are used to track motion and can be used to determine position and velocity. This can be either linear or rotary motion. Because the direction can be determined, very accurate measurements can be made.

They employ two outputs called A and B which are called quadrature outputs as they are 90 degrees out of phase. These signals are decoded to produce a count up pulse or a count down pulse. The A and B outputs are then read by the motion controller software.

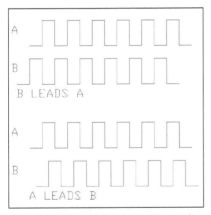

The A and B quadrature outputs of an incremental encoder.

A rotary encoder.

Other Motion I/O

Additional I/O can include limit switches, datum switches, position triggers, and position capture inputs. Limit switches provide information about the end of travel to avoid damage to the system. When a motion system reaches a limit switch, the typical response is for motion to come to a halt. Datum switches indicate the home position of the system and define a reference point.

In addition, limit switches are often used as ultimate or overtravel switches that disconnect power directly from the drive system. This is a safety feature that may be employed if the motion control risk assessment determines that protection from over-travel is required. These switches are usually wired independently of the motion controller to provide a level of redundancy.

A TER limit box.

A Telemecanique limit switch.

21 DATA COMMUNICATIONS

The application software will need to communicate with the motion controller, to pass information such as target position, speed and acceleration; also the motion controller will need to pass information back to the application software such as current position, speed and any fault conditions. This information is passed back and forth as data. The data is transmitted and received as little packets of information travelling at very high speed, such that the operator is unaware that the information is in fact taking a finite time to both be sent and received.

A modern automation console will use 'data communications' to achieve the above task, there are several methods in common use but ultimately they all achieve the same goal.

The methods in common use today are:
- Ethernet
- RS485
- CanBus
- ProfiBus

Ethernet is the type of communications often seen in offices and home networks and uses the Internet Protocol (IP) to send and receive information. It has the advantage that it is a well understood technology with many manufacturers producing hardware that is compatible with each other. If it has a disadvantage it is that occasionally it tends to freeze up if there is a data collision requiring a re-boot of the system.

RS485 is an older form of serial communications that is much simpler than Ethernet. The information being sent and received has to be defined between the sender and receiver. This has the advantage that only information that is actually required plus a small amount of addressing and error detecting is used but has the disadvantage that it becomes very vendor specific. It is a very robust form of data communication with any errors or data collisions being quickly discarded to the extent that the operator will be unaware that they have occurred.

CanBus or more fully Controller-area network (CAN or CAN-bus) is a computer network protocol and bus standard designed to allow microcontrollers and devices to communicate with each other without a host computer. It was designed specifically for automotive applications but is now also used in other areas including stage automation. Several problems have come to light over the years with CAN-Bus including the relatively large amount of information that has to be transmitted along with what is actually required, the need for specially designed receivers and transmitters, the relatively short distances that can be communicated over (at a decent speed) and difficult fault finding. It is therefore becoming less popular.

PROFIBUS (Process Field Bus) is a standard for field bus communication in automation technology and was first promoted in 1989 by BMBF (German department of education and research). It should not be confused with the PROFINET standard for industrial Ethernet. PROFIBUS is similar in some ways to CAN-Bus but has less of the drawbacks and is more widespread through the automation industry with many more manufacturers providing hardware and software.

Whichever type of data communications is being used, the main advantage is that a huge amount of data is travelling very quickly down only a few conductors. This has the advantage that if a fault does occur it can be traced quite quickly, but has the disadvantage that any fault usually results in complete communication breakdown.

The data that is transmitted from the application software on the console will have to be connected to every motion controller, either from a hub or by daisy-chaining. Each motion controller will have its own address, usually set by little DIP switches or software, such that it knows when it is being 'talked to' and will respond with its assigned address when 'talking back' to the application software. The application software, or a third-party communication interface, will sort out all the timing of messages and ensure that there are no data collisions and that all messages are responded to appropriately.

The further the data communications has to travel the more likely it is that the signal will become distorted or interfered with by noise. If nothing were done about this, then potentially erroneous information could be passed from the application software to the motion controller causing uncommanded motion. It is therefore important that precautions are taken to minimise any noise or distortion and that the information received is checked for errors.

Minimising noise and distortion can be achieved by using the correct data cable. The correct data cable will have the correct impedance, will have twisted-pair conductors and will be screened. The correct impedance will ensure that the cable is not introducing any more attenuation than is actually necessary. Twisted-pair conductors will help to cancel out any noise introduced and correct screening will help ensure that any noise is grounded before being borne onto the data conductors.

Error checking should be done by all stage automation equipment using data communications. Ethernet uses a system known as FCS (Frame Check Sequence), RS485 uses a Checksum method, CAN-Bus uses an ACK field in its data structure to detect transmission errors and PROFIBUS uses a Bus Check Error system.

DMX is similar to RS485 but is unidirectional and does not use error checking and therefore should not be used for stage automation.

22 RISK ASSESSMENT

The main purpose of risk assessment is to assess any potential safety risks and reduce those hazards to an acceptable level.

In simple terms there are only two factors to consider:

The severity of foreseeable injuries (ranging from a bruise to a fatality)

The probability of their occurrence.

There is little that can be done about the severity of an injury, but much can be done to reduce the probability of that injury. The stage automation engineer must look carefully at the initial design to assess the potential for avoiding or reducing as many hazards as possible.

Risk assessment falls into two broad types, the formal and the informal. The informal risk assessment is usually a brief list of the potential hazards and a corresponding list of what steps have been taken to reduce those risks. The formal risk assessment will be carried out in accordance with a particular standard adhering to a method of evaluating the risk and calculating the appropriate safety integrity level (SIL) and then using recognised methods of reducing the risk to an acceptable level.

The informal type of risk assessment has no place in stage automation and will not therefore be considered any further here.

The formal risk assessment is first carried out at the design stage, where all the envisioned risks are evaluated, and depending on which standard is being applied are each given a category or level. The main standards that tend to be applied are EN954-1, DIN19250 or IEC61508. The first two standards use a relatively easy tree-chart to assess risk and calculate a safety level. IEC61508 is a more complex standard that requires a more robust mathematical approach, but nevertheless results in a similar safety integrity level (SIL).

Extract from EN954-1: Risk Assessment chart

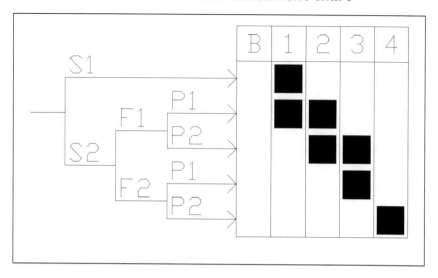

S **Severity of injury**
   S1   Slight (reversible)
   S2   Serious (non-reversible)

F **Frequency and exposure times**
   F1   Seldom and/or short exposure
   F2   Frequent to continuous and/or long exposure

P **Possibility of avoiding the hazard**
   P1   Possible under specific conditions
   P2   Less possible

The standard EN954-1 defines five categories for safety-related parts of control systems. The categories state the required behaviour of the controls in respect of resistance to faults.

Category B
The basic category. The occurrence of a fault can lead to loss of safety function.

Category 1

Improved resistance to faults is achieved predominantly by selection and application of components. This is achieved by using well-tried components and well-tried safety principles. The standard gives an interpretation of these terms in the context of this Standard;

Category 2

Improved performance is required. This is achieved by using all the principles stated in Category 1 together with designing the control system so that the safety-related functions are checked at suitable intervals by the machine control system. This check will be made at machine start-up and at other periods as determined by the risk assessment. After detection of a fault, a safe state will be maintained until the fault has been cleared.

Category 3

Improved so that a single fault will not lead to loss of a safety function. This requires the application of all the principles of previously mentioned categories together with the safety-related parts of the control system being designed so that a single fault in any of these parts does not lead to a loss of the safety function. Common mode faults need to be taken into account when the probability of such a fault occurring is significant. Whenever reasonably practical, the single fault should be detected at or before the next demand for the safety function. All faults do not require to be detected, thus an accumulation of undetected faults could lead to an unintended and thus hazardous situation at the machine.

Category 4

All faults will be detected and there will be protection against an accumulation of faults which needs to be specified. The safety-related parts of the control need to be designed so that a single fault does not lead to a loss of safety function and the single fault will be detected at or before the next demand for the safety function. If this is not possible, then and accumulation of faults must not lead to a loss of safety function. In practice the number of faults which need to be considered will vary considerably, for example in the case of complex microprocessor circuits, a large number of faults can exist but in a electro-hydraulic circuit, the consideration of three or so faults can be sufficient. If further faults occur as a result of the first single fault the first and all consequent faults shall be considered as a single fault. Common mode faults need to be taken into account by using, say, diversity, and special procedures introduced to identify such faults. This category of safety requires that when faults occur the safety function is always performed and the faults will be detected in time to prevent the loss of the safety function.

Once a SIL or risk category has been determined there are formal methods of ensuring that the design of the automation system provides the required level of risk reduction. These methods rely on good product selection, redundancy and monitoring. There are many products on the market such as emergency stop relays, safety edge, over speed monitors, safety limit switches and safety PLCs etc, that when correctly selected and configured ensure that the risk reduction requirement identified by the risk assessment has been adequately dealt with.

23 SAFETY STANDARDS

The standards prepared by the European standardisation bodies CEN and CENELEC are common to all European community countries. These standards were introduced in order to help machinery manufacturers conform to the requirements of the regulations (European Machinery Directive, EMD). Generally speaking, the authorities will assume that any machine manufactured to conform to the published European standards will comply with the Essential Health and Safety Requirements covered by those standards.

What this means is that the standards in themselves are not regulations, but by conforming to the standards will ensure compliance with the regulations. It is therefore imperative that the stage automation engineer has a good working knowledge of the regulations and the appropriate standards to apply.

The standards have been classified into three groups: A, B and C.

The A standards apply to all machinery and provide essential information for all machine builders. There are three standards that relate to stage machinery:

> EN 414
>
> EN 292 Parts 1 and 2
>
> EN 1050.

Once a safety integrity level or category has been established, there are guidelines within each standard as to how to reduce the risks. These guidelines may suggest simple redundancy, monitoring or complex dual channel safety devices. It is then incumbent upon the stage automation engineer to implement those risk reduction measures, in accordance with other safety standards, to ensure that the

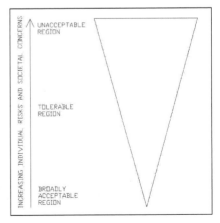

final design has had the risks reduced 'as low as reasonably practicable' (ALARP).

For a risk to be ALARP it must be possible to demonstrate that the cost involved in reducing the risk further would be grossly disproportionate to the benefit gained. The ALARP principle arises from the fact that it would be possible to spend infinite time, effort and money attempting to reduce a risk to zero. It should not be understood as simply a quantitive measure of benefit against detriment. It is more a best common practice of judgement of the balance of risk and benefit.

The risk assessment procedure is applied again after the installation is complete to ensure that no risks have been overlooked or inappropriately dealt with.

If an accident should occur even after these procedures have been applied, the stage automation system should be assessed again to establish whether any further risk reduction measures are appropriate.

It is only by carrying out a formal risk assessment and applying risk reduction measures to an established standard that a stage automation engineer can prove due diligence in the design of a stage automation system.

EN414

"Safety of machinery. Rules for drafting and presentation of safety standards".

In effect the standard for writing standards so that there is some conformity between them.

EN292 Parts 1 and 2

"Safety of machinery. Basic concepts, general principles for design"

This standard defines the concept of machinery safety and specifies the general principles and techniques to help machine designers achieve safety.

EN1050

"Safety of machinery. Principles for risk assessment".

This standard describes how to assess the risk of injury or damage to health, so that appropriate safety measures can be selected.

The B standards are sub-divided into two sections:

Group B1 covers safety aspects for design, e.g. electrical equipment, safety distances, safety related controls. These standards always apply.

Group B2 covers safety components and devices, e.g. light curtains, mechanical guards, emergency stop control. These standards are applied when required.

The C standards identify specific types or groups of machinery and inform manufacturers and users about the specific safety precautions they should take and safety devices they should use.

There is a new EN standard currently being discussed by CEN CWA25 working party specifically for theatre machinery. This is based largely on the existing German standard DIN 56950 and when this standard is eventually ratified it will become a C type standard. This should clear up some of the anomalies of attempting to apply industrial machinery safety standards in a theatre. Indeed, some theatre equipment is currently specifically excluded from the Machinery Directive, however by attempting to apply as many standards as possible, due diligence can be demonstrated.

Other standards bodies such as IEC, ISO and significantly the American national standards body ANSI are now reaching agreement with CEN and CENELEC in order to reach common, world-wide standards.

In addition to the above, there are numerous British Standards including BS7905-1, design of lifting equipment for performance, broadcast and similar applications as well as the *Technical Standards for Places of Entertainment* produced jointly by the Association of British Theatre Technicians (ABTT) and The District Surveyors Association. Although perhaps not directly concerned with stage automation these other standards do need to be considered and used in conjunction and sympathetically with the standards that do apply to produce an automation system that is as safe as possible.

24 ELECTRICAL STANDARDS

Since stage automation is basically an electrical control system there are more specific electrical standards to be considered, such as BS7671, EN418, EN60204-1, EN954-1, IEC61508 and DIN19250.

BS7671 are 'the IEE wiring regs', recently amended to the seventeenth edition and now known at the IET Wiring Regulations. These regulations provide valuable information concerning the electrical installation, especially with regard to cable types and sizes, earthing arrangements, equipotential bonding, overload protection and trunking.

EN418 Safety of Machinery. Emergency stop equipment, functional aspects. Principles for design. This is the specific standard for the design of emergency stop equipment. By using emergency stop equipment designed to this standard, configured in the correct way for the level of safety integrity required, as determined by the risk assessment, the appropriate emergency stop system is fairly easily designed.

EN60204-1 Safety of Machinery. Electrical equipment of machines. Specification for general requirements. This standard provides requirements and recommendations relating to the electrical equipment of machines so as to promote safety of persons and property, consistency of control response, and ease of maintenance. It applies to electrical, electronic and programmable electronic equipment and systems to machines not portable by hand while working, including groups of machines working together in a co-ordinated manner.

EN954-1 Safety of Machinery. Safety related parts of control systems. Part 1: general principles for design. This standard sets out a procedure for the selection and design of safety measures. The procedure contains five steps:

1. Hazard analysis and risk assessment
2. Decide measures to reduce risk
3. Specify safety requirements to be provided by the safety related parts of the control system.
4. Design
5. Validation.

EN954-1 also provides a list of typical safety functions:

1. Stop

2. Emergency stop

3. Manual reset

4. Start and re-start

5. Response time

6. Safety related parameters

7. Local control functions

8. Fluctuations, loss and restoration of power sources

9. Muting

10. Manual suspension of safety functions

Categories that define the behaviour of the safety related parts of the control system are also specified. The categories are B, 1, 2, 3 and 4 with category B being the lowest with no special measures for safety and Category 4 being the highest where no single fault shall lead to a loss of safety and the single fault shall be detected, as detailed in chapter 22.

IEC61508 is an international standard developed by the International Electrotechnical Commission (IEC). The standard consists of the following parts under the general title of 'Functional safety of electrical/electronic/ programmable electronic (E/E/EP) safety related systems":

1. General requirements

2. Requirements for E/E/EP safety related systems

3. Software requirements

4. Definitions and abbreviations

5. Examples of methods for the determination of safety integrity levels

6. Guidance on the application of IEC 61508 parts 2 and 3

IEC61508 should be used to develop safety related systems for applications requiring more complex systems.

DIN19250 is a German DIN standard also for E/E/EP safety related systems that defines the relationship with risk and the German Requirement Class (AK). The standard uses a graph, similar to EN954-1, but with six levels. Until the release of IEC61508, the TUV in Germany certified E/E/EP safety related systems to DIN19250, now however IEC61508 is used instead. Indeed IEC61508 part 2 has incorporated many of the DIN standard requirements and part 5 has incorporated an example of the risk graph that is similar to the DIN19250 standard.

25 EMC

Stage automation by necessity employs AC motor inverters, servo amplifiers, motion controllers, computers, encoders and long cables. AC motor inverters and servo amplifiers are electromagnetically noisy, computers; motion controllers and encoders are electromagnetically sensitive and the cables for both parts of the system are necessarily in the same vicinity. It is therefore imperative that a stage automation system employs the highest possible standards with regard to electromagnetic interference both for its own reliability and also to prevent interference to neighbouring systems such as lighting, sound and AV. In addition there are regulations known as the EMC Directive governing the design and use of electrical equipment such that no equipment will interfere with other equipment.

Excerpt from the EMC Directive

Directive 2004/108/EC of the European Parliament and of the Council, of 15 December 2004, on the approximation of the Laws of Member States relating to electromagnetic compatibility governs on the one hand the electromagnetic emissions of this equipment in order to ensure that, in its intended use, such equipment does not disturb radio and telecommunication as well as other equipment. In the other the Directive also governs the immunity of such equipment to interference and seeks to ensure that this equipment is not disturbed by radio emissions normally present used as intended.

The main objective of the EMC Directive is thus to regulate the compatibility of equipment regarding EMC. In order to achieve this objective, provisions have been put in place so that:

Equipment (apparatus and fixed installations) needs to comply with the requirements of the EMC Directive when it is placed on the market and/or taken into service;

The application of good engineering practice is required for fixed installations, with the possibility for the competent authorities of Member States to impose measures if non-compliances are established

In order to comply with the EMC Directive, a necessity for all the reasons just outlined as well as being required for the CE mark, there are several key standards supporting the Directive:

EN50081-1 Electromagnetic compatibility – Generic emission standard.Part 1. Residential, commercial and light industry.

EN50081-2 Electromagnetic compatibility – Generic emission standard. Part 2. Industrial Environment.

EN50082-1 Electromagnetic compatibility – Generic immunity standard. Part 1. Residential, commercial and light industry.

EN50082-2 Electromagnetic compatibility – Generic immunity standard. Part 2. Industrial Environment.

IEC1000 Good EMC practice for installers.

All of the equipment that is incorporated into a stage automation system should comply with the above standards in addition to being designed and assembled in accordance with good practice. If all of the recommendations are followed there should not be a problem with EMC.

Immunity of Sensitive Circuits

The following list indicates the relative sensitivity of a variety of electronic circuits found in stage automation control systems.

Not Sensitive

Purely electrical circuits, relays, contactors and electromechanical items such as brakes.

Not Significantly Sensitive

Many electronic systems are insensitive to drive emissions. Computers, PLCs, all digital electronic circuits and analogue circuits using levels over 1 Volt are unlikely to be disturbed unless they include components which fall into the next category or are installed in such a way that they are closely coupled to drive emissions.

Sensitive

Analogue measuring circuits using low levels such as speed signals below

1 Volt, strain gauges and similar equipment, especially if the connections are very long or unscreened.

Digital data links, only if unscreened. Conventional RS232, RS485 and fast links such as Ethernet have good immunity when correctly installed with high screening cable.

Proximity sensors which rely on high frequency oscillators, particularly capacitance types.

Motor Cable

The only certain way of preventing emission from the motor cable is to screen it. The screen should be connected to both the drive earth and the motor frame. It is important that the connection be made at both ends to minimise the external magnetic field. Screened cable is also very effective in ensuring that the RF current which flows through the motor stray capacitance to the motor frame returns along the screen to the drive and not by stray paths through the metal structure to which the motor is attached.

Control Circuit

Most drives have electrically isolated control circuits. The control circuit should preferably be earthed at one point in the system, remote from the drive. This means that the "0V" connection should be earthed at the equipment to which the control lines are connected.

Screening of Sensitive Circuits

The main function of a screen is to prevent capacitive pick-up from the electric field of an adjacent circuit where the voltage is changing at a high rate. In order to achieve this it is only necessary for the screen to be earthed at one point. The induced current flows along the screen to earth without disturbing the circuit.

Supply Filter

A filter should be fitted in the mains supply line to a drive. Drives generate high levels of medium order harmonics which may effect sensitive circuits connected to the same supply. In addition the switching frequency of the drive should be at the lowest acceptable.

26 LVD

Part of the European Machinery Directive (EMD) is the Low Voltage Directive (LVD) and stage automation control systems have to comply with it. The purpose of the directive is to ensure that people cannot be electrocuted.

The LVD affects manufacturers, importers, representatives, suppliers of second hand equipment, equipment hire companies and even people who let accommodation containing electrical equipment.

The regulation says that all electrical equipment must be safe, that there should be no risk in using it, apart from those residual risks that have been reduced to a minimum. These must carry warnings either on the equipment if practical, or in the operating instructions.

Equipment must be manufactured in accordance with good engineering practice. It must be safe when connected to the electrical supply system by providing a level of protection against electric shock which relies on insulation and earthing or other means which will achieve the level of safety.

It is normal for stage automation control systems to have their control voltage at 24 Volts DC, so that there is no risk of injury from this part of the control system. In addition AC motor inverters retain their high voltage DC link for some time after switching off because of the storage effect of the electrolytic capacitors and so a warning to this effect is mandatory for compliance to the low voltage directive.

Compliance with the Low Voltage Directive is law and mandatory in most European countries including the UK. An excerpt from the introduction is given here.

The Low Voltage Directive (73/23/EEC) as amended 93/68/EEC

The Electrical Equipment (Safety) Regulations (LVD) applies to all electrical equipment designed for use with a voltage rating of between 50 and 1000 V AC and between 75 and 1500 V DC. Plugs and Sockets are covered by separate legislation namely the Plugs and Sockets etc.

(Safety) Regulations 1994 (SI 1994 No. 1768). Broadly, the scope the LVD covers consumer and capital goods designed to operate within those voltage limits, including in particular electrical appliances, lighting equipment including ballasts, switch gear and control gear, electric wiring, appliance couplers and cord sets, electrical installation equipment, etc. and electrical equipment intended for incorporation into other equipment such as transformers and motors.

The Directive covers all risks arising from the use of electrical equipment, including not just electrical ones but also mechanical, chemical (such as, in particular, emission of aggressive substances), health aspects of noise and vibrations, and ergonomic aspects as far as ergonomic requirements are necessary to protect against hazards in the sense of the Directive. The LVD lays down eleven "safety objectives", which represent the essential requirements of this Directive.

Products are presumed to conform to the safety objectives of the LVD where the equipment has been manufactured in accordance with a harmonized standard. Alternatively, the manufacturer may construct the product in conformity with the essential requirements (safety objectives) of the LVD, without applying harmonised, international or national standards. In such a case the product will not benefit from presumption of conformity and therefore the manufacturer must include in the technical documentation a description of the solutions adopted to satisfy the safety aspects of the Directive.

27 EMERGENCY STOP

The emergency stop in a stage automation system has to be able to stop all the controlled equipment in a safe way. This means that the equipment definitely has to stop, obvious perhaps, but also that it stops safely. For instance, if a fast turning revolve were stopped suddenly, anyone standing on it would fall over. This could potentially cause a greater injury to a person than was originally the case before the emergency stop was actuated. Similarly a heavy load on a fly bar, if stopped suddenly, may put undue strain on a piece of scenery that might then fall to the stage. Therefore the emergency stop first has to decelerate the motor to a stop in as quick a time as can be safely implemented followed by an assured disconnection of power and application of brakes.

The emergency stop system has to be designed and manufactured to the relevant SIL or risk category as defined by the risk assessment of the equipment. Generally, this is Category 3 or 4 or SIL3 for stage automation systems. The implementation of such an emergency stop system is relatively straightforward and there is not much to be gained for implementing a lower category emergency stop system as the costs and hardware are quite similar.

The heart of an emergency stop system is the emergency stop relay. There are several manufacturers that produce emergency stop relays and by and large they all tend to follow the same principles. Firstly, a category 3 or 4 emergency stop relay will have terminals for two normally closed contacts on the emergency stop button. This ensures that there is redundancy in the control circuit, such that if one contact were to fail the other would surely work. This function is then checked by the emergency stop relay such that if there were any fault it would be detected and the emergency stop relay would not energise. In addition, the emergency stop relay has at lease one safety output contact, but more usually it has two or three safety contacts and where a deceleration period is required it would also have a timed safety contact output. The output safety contactors would be in the moving circuits of the motion control and/or drives and the timed safety contact would be in the prime power and brake circuits. Any slave relays and contactors would be positively guided and their contacts would also be monitored by the emergency stop relay, so that any fault would be detected and the emergency stop relay would not energise.

Once the emergency stop relay is energised the motion control system is in control of the drives and thus the motors. But if the emergency stop relay is de-energised no motion is possible from the drives regardless of whether the motion control system is commanding a move or not. A good motion control system will know the status of the emergency stop and will not attempt a move when it is de-energised. In addition, there are often several emergency stop buttons around a theatre, and all buttons should stop all equipment so that there is no confusion. Ideally the operator should be able to distinguish which button has been pressed and be able to reset the emergency stop from their control position once the reason for the emergency stop has been established.

A Telemecanique emergeny stop relay.

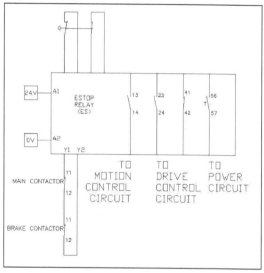

Diagram of an emergency stop circuit.

ADDENDUM APRIL 2011

Transition from EN954-1 to EN ISO 13849

Chapter 24 described risk assessment in accordance with EN954-1, however that standard is about to be withdrawn and replaced by EN ISO 13849-1: 2008. In order to comply with the Machinery Directive from December 2011 onwards, the new standard will have to be applied.

The old standard produced safety categories B, 1, 2, 3 and 4. The new standard will produce Performance Levels (PL) a, b, c, d, and e. However the old EN954-1 categories are still used to describe the architecture of control systems in the new standard, which is why Chapter 24 has not been removed.

The new standard requires reliability data for the main parts of the safety control system, the diagnostic coverage (DC) of the system must be assessed and there must be protection against common cause faults (CCF), systematic faults and, where relevant, there are specific requirements for software.

In the first instance the various risks are evaluated in accordance with EN ISO 14121, which means that each risk has to be evaluated taking into consideration not just the basic hazard but also noting the location of the hazard, the mode of the machine, i.e. normal use, maintenance, day time, show time, there should be a description of what is causing the hazard and a description of what the hazard reduction measure will be.

Then each risk in each of the locations and modes identified using EN ISO 14121 are assessed using a risk graph that is similar to the old risk graph under EN954-1 but will produce a Performance Level Requirement (PLr) a, b, c, d or e instead of a Category B, 1, 2, 3 or 4.

S1   Slight injury
S2   Serious injury
F1   Rare exposure/short exposure
F2   Frequent exposure/long exposure
P1   Possibility of elimination
P2   No elimination possible

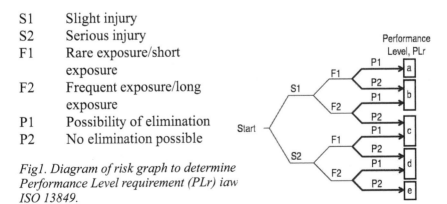

Fig1. Diagram of risk graph to determine Performance Level requirement (PLr) iaw ISO 13849.

Once the performance level requirement is determined, the control system reduction measure has to be assessed using EN ISO 13849-1 to ensure that the hazard has been reduced properly.

This is done by first splitting the safety part of the control system into three sub-sections; the input section, the logic section and then the output section. If we take an emergency stop system as an example, the emergency stop buttons would be the input sub-section, the emergency stop relay would the logic sub-section and the contactors that switch power to the drive system would be the output sub-section.

Each of these sub-sections is then assessed for reliability, architecture, diagnostic coverage and common cause failure and systematic failure. There is then a calculation of each sub-section to work out its 'average probability of dangerous failures per hour' (PFHd), and these three scores are added together to get a total PHFd. This final score will then match one of the five performance levels PL, if it meets or exceeds the original performance level requirement PLr then the control system reduction measure has been calculated as being sufficient. If the assessed PL does not meet the original PLr then it has failed to meet the required standard and the design will have to revised, perhaps by increasing from a single channel safety system to a dual channel safety system, then reassessed until it does meet the performance level requirement.

In order to each assess sub-section, various data is required to perform the calculation. The first piece of data is the 'Mean time to dangerous failure (years)' (MTTFd). This is a figure that the manufacturers of the safety components should be able to provide. A typical value for an emergency stop relay is 100 years, which does not mean that it will take 100 years for an emergency stop relay to fail, it is more like if there are 100 emergency stop relays, one of them might fail in a dangerous way in one year. The next figure for the calculation is the architecture assessment; this uses the old EN954-1 category system to assess how the safety control system architecture is designed. Therefore a cat 1 system would rely on well tried and tested components, a cat 2 system might have some test on start-up, a cat 3 system might have a redundant channel with monitoring and cat 4 system might have complex system monitoring. The next figure is the diagnostic coverage (DC); this is the amount of monitoring that is going on. An emergency stop system that is monitoring the state of itself and perhaps any contactors that it is controlling would be deemed to have a high DC, whereas perhaps a simple guard switch that has no monitoring would have a low DC. These figures are then checked using a performance level calculator, graph or specialist software to determine the 'average probability of dangerous failure per hour' PHFd. Once the PHFd for each sub-section is calculated and added together, a total PHFd value is then compared with the table below and a performance level is determined.

Average Probability of dangerous failures per hour	Performance Level PL
$\geq 10^{-5}$ to $<10^{-4}$	a
$\geq 3 \times 10^{-6}$ to $<10^{-5}$	b
$\geq 10^{-6}$ to 3.1×10^{-6}	c
$\geq 10^{-7}$ to $<10^{-6}$	d
$\geq 10^{-8}$ to $<10^{-7}$	e

In addition to the above calculations, common cause failure (CCF) analysis has to be undertaken. A common cause failure is where a single cause such as environmental, training or incompetence might cause a dangerous failure. This is done by using the following table and attaining a score of at least 65 to claim conformance.

No	Measure against CCF	Score
1	Separation/segregation	15
2	Diversity	20
3	Design/Application/Experience	20
4	Assessment/Analysis	5
5	Competence/Training	5
6	Environmental	35

Finally systematic failure has to be considered. Typical systematic failures are software design errors, hardware design errors and requirement specification errors. Systematic failures are not the same as random errors, which would normally occur when hardware has degraded. Systematic errors can be tested for and eliminated.

It is also possible under the new standard to declare that a particular fault is so unlikely as to be excluded. However, a claim of this type has to be backed up with very detailed justification.

GLOSSARY

Absolute (encoder)
Encoder output has a unique digital code for each distinct angle of the shaft.

AC
An electric current whose magnitude and direction vary cyclically (usually a sine wave).

Acceleration
An increase in speed, more specifically the instantaneous rate of change of velocity (speed and direction) measured in SI units as meters per second squared. In stage automation more usually given as a ramp time from standstill to top speed in time only.

Asynchronous (motor)
A motor whose rotor is designed to slip in relation to the rotating field and create torque.

Automation (stage)
The use of control systems to control stage machinery, reducing the need for human intervention.

Axis
A term to refer to the combination of motion controller, drive, motor/gearbox, winch and peripheral components such as limit switches and encoder but does not include the actual scenery.

Brake
A brake is a device for slowing or stopping the motion of a machine, or alternatively a device to restrain it from starting to move again.

Capacitor
A capacitor is an electrical/electronic device that can store energy in the electric field between a pair of conductors (called "plates").

Chopping (frequency)
The carrier frequency of an AC Motor inverter that is modulated to provide pseudo three phase output.

Closed-loop
Proportional, integral and derivative (PID) control loop designed to attempt to correct error between measured position (in stage automation) and desired set-point.

Command
A command is a directive to the computer program to perform a specific task.

Contactor
A contactor is an electrically controlled switch (relay) used for switching a power circuit. A contactor is activated by a control input which is a lower voltage/current than that which the contactor is switching.

Counterweight (flying)

A counterweight fly system is a system of ropes, counterweights and pulleys, within a theatre designed to allow a technical crew to quickly move set pieces, on and off stage by 'flying' them in from a large opening above the stage known as a fly tower, or fly gallery.

Cue

A theatrical cue is the trigger for an action to be carried out at a specific time. It is generally associated with theatre and the film industry. They can be necessary for a lighting change or effect, a sound effect, or some sort of stage or set movement/change.

Cycloconverter

A cycloconverter or a cycloinverter converts an AC waveform, such as the mains supply, to another AC waveform of a lower frequency, synthesising the output waveform from segments of the AC supply without an intermediate direct-current link.

Datum

A reference point to fix the position of a piece of machinery (esp. Revolve).

DC

Direct current is the unidirectional flow of electric charge, distinguishing it from alternating current (AC).

Dead

A recorded position of a piece of scenery.

Deadman (handle) (DMH)

A safety switch that requires human contact to energise, usually to initiate and maintain motor control.

Deceleration

A decrease in speed, more specifically the instantaneous rate of change of velocity (speed and direction) measured in SI units as meters per second squared. In stage automation more usually given as a ramp time from top speed to standstill in time only.

Demand (position)

The required final (or intermediate) position of a piece of scenery, given as a command from the computer program, translated as the target by the motion controller.

Diode

A diode is a two-terminal device and mostly used for their unidirectional current property. The most common function of a diode is to allow an electric current to pass in one direction (called the forward biased condition) and to block it in the opposite direction (the reverse biased condition).

DOL

A direct on line starter, often abbreviated DOL starter, is a widely-used starting method of electric motors.

Drive

A drive is an electronic device to provide power to a motor or servo.

Emergency Stop
A safety switch that brings all moving equipment to a controlled stop and then after a short delay removes power from motor power circuits.

End of Travel (limit switch)
Most systems will have software and hardware limits to prevent movement beyond the capabilities of the stage machinery.

EU
European Union.

Field (frequency)
The rotating electromagnetic force in an AC motor that causes the rotor to rotate.

Fit-Up
The period of time when a stage production is installed into a theatre, prior to technical rehearsal.

Flux Vector
Provides more precise speed control of a motor from an AC motor inverter.

FLC
Full Load Current. The greatest current that a circuit or motor is designed to carry under specified conditions.

Follow on
A term (orig Cricket) to describe the following of one cue by another automatically.

Frequency
Frequency is defined as a number of cycles, or periods, per unit time. In SI units, the unit of frequency is Hertz (Hz), For example, 1Hz means that an event repeats once per second, 2Hz is twice per second, and so on.

Group
A collection of Axes (pl. Axis) that are grouped together in the application software, either loosely or locked.

Hoist
A hoist is a device used for lifting or lowering a load by means of a drum or lift-wheel around which rope or chain wraps. It may be manually operated or electrically driven and may use chain, fiber or wire rope as its lifting medium.

Hydraulics
Hydraulic machines use fluid power to do work. In this type of machine, high pressure hydraulic fluid is transmitted throughout the machine to various hydraulic motors and hydraulic cylinders. The fluid is controlled directly or automatically by control valves and distributed through hoses and tubes. The popularity of hydraulic machinery is due to the very large amount of power that can be transferred through small tubes and flexible hoses, and the high power density and wide array of actuators that can make use of this power.

Incremental (encoder)

An incremental rotary encoder, also known as a quadrature encoder or a relative rotary encoder, has two outputs called quadrature outputs. The incremental rotary encoder is the most widely used of all rotary encoders due to its low cost: only two sensors are required.

Jog (speed)

A motor speed that is fixed, often used as a 'creep' speed.

Ladder (logic)

Ladder logic is a philosophy of drawing electrical logic schematics. It is now a graphical language very popular for programming Programmable Logic Controllers (PLCs). It was originally invented to describe logic made from relays. The name is based on the observation that programs in this language resemble ladders, with two vertical "rails" and a series of horizontal "rungs" between them.

Motion Controller

A motion controller controls the position and/or velocity of machines.

Motor

An electric motor uses electrical energy to produce mechanical energy.

Open-loop

An open-loop controller, also called a non-feedback controller, is a type of controller which computes its input into a system using only the current state and its model of the system. A characteristic of the open-loop controller is that it does not use feedback to determine if its input has achieved the desired goal. This means that the system does not observe the output of the processes that it is controlling.

Over load

A situation where an electrical or mechanical machine or system is subjected to a greater load than it was designed for.

Over travel (limit switch)

A safety switch that is struck by the machine when it has inadvertently travelled too far. Normally this will remove motor power immediately and release the brake signal. Also called Ultimate limit switch.

Parameter

The term parameter refers to an individual measured or set item in a motion controller, drive or application software. For instance; speed, gain, software limits, acceleration and demand position are all parameters.

Periactoid

A three sided tower, often revolving.

Positional (error)

Positional error is the difference between where an axis actually is and where it should be during motion. This value is normally multiplied by a constant along with other signals to produce the correcting signal in a closed loop system.

Profile (motion)

The motion profile is the shape of the motion path, usually trapezoidal.

PLC

A programmable logic controller (PLC) or programmable controller is a digital computer used for automation of industrial processes, such as control of machinery on factory assembly lines. Unlike general-purpose computers, the PLC is designed for multiple inputs and output arrangements, extended temperature ranges, immunity to electrical noise, and resistance to vibration and impact. Programs to control machine operation are typically stored in battery-backed or non-volatile memory. A PLC is an example of a real time system since output results must be produced in response to input conditions within a bounded time, otherwise unintended operation will result.

Ramp

Ramp is the integral of a step function. Often used in stage automation to describe acceleration and deceleration in time units only.

RCD

A residual current device (RCD), or residual current circuit breaker (RCCB), is an electrical wiring device that disconnects a circuit whenever it detects that the electric current is not balanced between the live phase conductor and the neutral conductor. Such an imbalance is sometimes caused by current leakage through the body of a person who is grounded and accidentally touching the energized part of the circuit. A lethal shock can result from these conditions; RCDs are designed to disconnect quickly enough to mitigate the harm caused by such shocks.

Redundancy

Redundancy in stage automation is the duplication of critical components of a system with the intention of increasing reliability of the system, usually in the case of a backup or fail-safe.

Relay

A relay is an electrical switch that opens and closes under the control of another electrical circuit. In the original form, the switch is operated by an electromagnet to open or close one or many sets of contacts.

Repertory

A repertory theatre can be a theatre in which a resident company presents works from a specified repertoire, usually in alternation or rotation.

Resolver

A resolver is a type of rotary electrical transformer used for measuring degrees of rotation.

Revolve

A revolve is a motorised rotating stage, usually circular. (US. Turntable).

RPM

Revolutions per minute, motor speeds are often given in RPM.

Semiconductor

A semiconductor is a solid material that has electrical conductivity in between that of a conductor and that of an insulator.

Single-Phase

Single-phase electric power refers to the distribution of alternating current (AC) electric power using a system in which all the voltages of the supply vary in unison. A single-phase supply connected to an alternating current electric motor does not produce a revolving magnetic field; single-phase motors need additional circuits for starting.

Slip

Slip is the difference in speed between the frequency supplied to an induction motor and rotor shaft speed.

Speed

Speed is the rate of motion, or equivalently the rate of change in position, often expressed as distance d traveled per unit of time t. Speed is a scalar quantity with dimensions distance/time; the equivalent vector quantity to speed is known as velocity.

Switchgear

The term switchgear refers to the combination of electrical disconnects, fuses and/or circuit breakers used to isolate electrical equipment.

Synchronous (motor)

A motor whose rotor rotates in synchrony with the oscillating field.

Target (position)

The target is the destination that the motion controller is aiming for, usually the same as the demand command given by the application software plus tolerances.

Three-Phase

Three-phase electric power systems have at least three conductors carrying voltage waveforms that are $2\pi/3$ radians (120°, 1/3 of a cycle in-phase) offset in time.

Traction

Traction refers to the friction between a drive member and the surface it moves upon, where the friction is used to provide motion.

Track

A horizontal movement on stage, e.g. stage wagon, truck or curtain.

Trajectory

Trajectory is the path a moving object follows. A trajectory can be described mathematically either by the geometry (e.g. trapezoidal) of the path, or as the position of the object over time.

Trapezoidal

A trapezoid is a quadrilateral that has at least one pair of parallel lines for sides. The motion profile or trajectory in motion control is often trapezoidal. ⬦

Torque

A torque (τ) (also called a moment) is a vector that measures the tendency of a force to rotate an object about some axis (center). The magnitude of a torque is defined as the product of a force and the length of the lever arm (radius). Just as a force is a push or a pull, a torque can be thought of as a twist. The SI unit for torque is Newton meters (Nm).

Turntable

See Revolve.

Ultimate (limit switch)

See over travel.

Velocity

See Speed, Velocity is similar to speed but with direction explicitly defined.

Welded (contact)

A fault condition in a relay (or contactor) where the contact has stuck short circuit. Force guided safety relays are used with monitoring where this fault condition may be dangerous.

Winch

A winch is a mechanical device that is used to pull in (wind up) or let out (wind out) or otherwise adjust the "tension" of a rope or wire rope. It can be used for both hoisting and tracking.

ENTERTAINMENT TECHNOLOGY PRESS

FREE SUBSCRIPTION SERVICE

Keeping Up To Date with

Stage Automation

Entertainment Technology titles are continually up-dated, and all major changes and additions are listed in date order in the relevant dedicated area of the publisher's website. Simply go to the front page of www.etnow.com and click on the BOOKS button. From there you can locate the title and be connected through to the latest information and services related to the publication.

The author of the title welcomes comments and suggestions about the book and can be contacted by email at: anton@avw.co.uk

Titles Published by Entertainment Technology Press

ABC of Theatre Jargon *Francis Reid* **£9.95** ISBN 1904031099
This glossary of theatrical terminology explains the common words and phrases that are used in normal conversation between actors, directors, designers, technicians and managers.

Aluminium Structures in the Entertainment Industry *Peter Hind* **£24.95**
ISBN 1904031064
Aluminium Structures in the Entertainment Industry aims to educate the reader in all aspects of the design and safe usage of temporary and permanent aluminium structures specific to the entertainment industry – such as roof structures, PA towers, temporary staging, etc.

AutoCAD 2010 – A Handbook for Theatre Users *David Ripley* **£24.95** ISBN 9781904031611
From 'Setting Up' to 'Drawing in Three Dimensions' via 'Drawings Within Drawings', this compact and fully illustrated guide to AutoCAD covers everything from the basics to full colour rendering and remote plotting. Title completely revised in June 2010.

Automation in the Entertainment Industry – A User's Guide *Mark Ager and John Hastie* **£29.95** ISBN 9781904031581
In the last 15 years, there has been a massive growth in the use of automation in entertainment, especially in theatres, and it is now recognised as its own discipline. However, it is still only used in around 5% of theatres worldwide. In the next 25 years, given current growth patterns, that figure will rise to 30%. This will mean that the majority of theatre personnel, including directors, designers, technical staff, actors and theatre management, will come into contact with automation for the first time at some point in their careers. This book is intended to provide insights and practical advice from those who use automation, to help the first-time user understand the issues and avoid the pitfalls in its implementation. In the past, theatre automation was seen by many as a complex, unreliable and expensive toy, not for general use. The aim of this book is to dispel that myth.

Basics – A Beginner's Guide to Lighting Design *Peter Coleman* **£9.95** ISBN 1904031412
The fourth in the author's 'Basics' series, this title covers the subject area in four main sections: The Concept, Practical Matters, Related Issues and The Design Into Practice. In an area that is difficult to be definitive, there are several things that cross all the boundaries of all lighting design and it's these areas that the author seeks to help with.

Basics – A Beginner's Guide to Special Effects *Peter Coleman* **£9.95** ISBN 1904031331
This title introduces newcomers to the world of special effects. It describes all types of special effects including pyrotechnic, smoke and lighting effects, projections, noise machines, etc. It places emphasis on the safe storage, handling and use of pyrotechnics.

Basics – A Beginner's Guide to Stage Lighting *Peter Coleman* **£9.95** ISBN 190403120X
This title does what it says: it introduces newcomers to the world of stage lighting. It will not teach the reader the art of lighting design, but will teach beginners much about the 'nuts and bolts' of stage lighting.

Basics: A Beginner's Guide to Stage Management *Peter Coleman* **£7.95**
ISBN 9781904031475
The fifth in Peter Coleman's popular 'Basics' series, this title provides a practical insight into, and the definition of, the role of stage management. Further chapters describe Cueing or 'Calling' the Show (the Prompt Book), and the Hardware and Training for Stage Management. This is a book about people and systems, without which most of the technical equipment used by others in the performance workplace couldn't function.

Basics – A Beginner's Guide to Stage Sound *Peter Coleman* **£9.95** ISBN 1904031277
This title does what it says: it introduces newcomers to the world of stage sound. It will not teach the reader the art of sound design, but will teach beginners much about the background to sound reproduction in a theatrical environment.

Building Better Theaters *Michael Mell* **£16.95** 1904031404
A title within our Consultancy Series, this book describes the process of designing a theater, from the initial decision to build through to opening night. Michael Mell's book provides a step-by-step guide to the design and construction of performing arts facilities. Chapters discuss: assembling your team, selecting an architect, different construction methods, the architectural design process, construction of the theater, theatrical systems and equipment, the stage, backstage, the auditorium, ADA requirements and the lobby. Each chapter clearly describes what to expect and how to avoid surprises. It is a must-read for architects, planners, performing arts groups, educators and anyone who may be considering building or renovating a theater.

Carry on Fading
Francis Reid **£20.00** ISBN 9781904031642
This is a record of five of the best years of my life. Years so good that the only downside is the pangs of guilt at enjoying such contentment in a world full of misery induced by greed, envy and imposed ideologies. Fortunately my DNA is high on luck, optimism and blessing counting. *Francis Reid.*

Case Studies in Crowd Management
Chris Kemp, Iain Hill, Mick Upton, Mark Hamilton **£16.95** ISBN 9781904031482
This important work has been compiled from a series of research projects carried out by the staff of the Centre for Crowd Management and Security Studies at Buckinghamshire Chilterns University College, and seminar work carried out in Berlin and Groningen with partner Yourope. It includes case studies, reports and a crowd management safety plan for a major outdoor rock concert, safe management of rock concerts utilising a triple barrier safety system and pan-European Health & Safety Issues.

Case Studies in Crowd Management, Security and Business Continuity
Chris Kemp, Patrick Smith **£24.95** ISBN 9781904031635
The creation of good case studies to support work in progress and to give answers to those seeking guidance in their quest to come to terms with perennial questions is no easy task. The first Case Studies in Crowd Management book focused mainly on a series of festivals and events that had a number of issues which required solving. This book focuses on a

series of events that had major issues that impacted on the every day delivery of the events researched.

Close Protection – The Softer Skills *Geoffrey Padgham* **£11.95** ISBN 1904031390
This is the first educational book in a new 'Security Series' for Entertainment Technology Press, and it coincides with the launch of the new 'Protective Security Management' Foundation Degree at Buckinghamshire Chilterns University College (BCUC). The author is a former full-career Metropolitan Police Inspector from New Scotland Yard with 27 years' experience of close protection (CP). For 22 of those years he specialised in operations and senior management duties with the Royalty Protection Department at Buckingham Palace, followed by five years in the private security industry specialising in CP training design and delivery. His wealth of protection experience comes across throughout the text, which incorporates sound advice and exceptional practical guidance, subtly separating fact from fiction. This publication is an excellent form of reference material for experienced operatives, students and trainees.

A Comparative Study of Crowd Behaviour at Two Major Music Events
Chris Kemp, Iain Hill, Mick Upton **£7.95** ISBN 1904031250
A compilation of the findings of reports made at two major live music concerts, and in particular crowd behaviour, which is followed from ingress to egress.

Control Freak *Wayne Howell* **£28.95** ISBN 9781904031550
Control Freak is the second book by Wayne Howell. It provides an in depth study of DMX512 and the new RDM (Remote Device Management) standards. The book is aimed at both users and developers and provides a wealth of real world information based on the author's twenty year experience of lighting control.

Copenhagen Opera House *Richard Brett and John Offord* **£32.00** ISBN 1904031420
Completed in a little over three years, the Copenhagen Opera House opened with a royal gala performance on 15th January 2005. Built on a spacious brown-field site, the building is a landmark venue and this book provides the complete technical background story to an opera house set to become a benchmark for future design and planning. Sixteen chapters by relevant experts involved with the project cover everything from the planning of the auditorium and studio stage, the stage engineering, stage lighting and control and architectural lighting through to acoustic design and sound technology plus technical summaries.

Electrical Safety for Live Events *Marco van Beek* **£16.95** ISBN 1904031285
This title covers electrical safety regulations and good pracitise pertinent to the entertainment industries and includes some basic electrical theory as well as clarifying the "do's and don't's" of working with electricity.

Entertainment in Production Volume 1: 1994-1999 *Rob Halliday* **£24.95**
ISBN 9781904031512

Entertainment in Production Volume 2: 2000-2006 *Rob Halliday* **£24.95**
ISBN 9781904031529
Rob Halliday has a dual career as a lighting designer/programmer and author and in these

two volumes he provides the intriguing but comprehensive technical background stories behind the major musical productions and other notable projects spanning the period 1994 to 2005. Having been closely involved with the majority of the events described, the author is able to present a first-hand and all-encompassing portrayal of how many of the major shows across the past decade came into being. From *Oliver!* and *Miss Saigon* to *Mamma Mia!* and *Mary Poppins*, here the complete technical story unfolds. The books, which are profusely illustrated, are in large part an adapted selection of articles that first appeared in the magazine *Lighting&Sound International*.

Entertainment Technology Yearbook 2008 *John Offord* **£14.95** ISBN 9781904031543
The new Entertainment Technology Yearbook 2008 covers the year 2007 and includes picture coverage of major industry exhibitions in Europe compiled from the pages of Entertainment Technology magazine and the etnow.com website, plus articles and pictures of production, equipment and project highlights of the year. Also included is a major European Trade Directory that will be regularly updated on line. A new edition will be published each year at the ABTT Theatre Show in London in June.

The Exeter Theatre Fire *David Anderson* **£24.95** ISBN 1904031137
This title is a fascinating insight into the events that led up to the disaster at the Theatre Royal, Exeter, on the night of September 5th 1887. The book details what went wrong, and the lessons that were learned from the event.

Fading Light – A Year in Retirement *Francis Reid* **£14.95** ISBN 1904031358
Francis Reid, the lighting industry's favourite author, describes a full year in retirement. "Old age is much more fun than I expected," he says. Fading Light describes visits and experiences to the author's favourite theatres and opera houses, places of relaxation and re-visits to scholarly institutions.

Focus on Lighting Technology *Richard Cadena* **£17.95** ISBN 1904031145
This concise work unravels the mechanics behind modern performance lighting and appeals to designers and technicians alike. Packed with clear, easy-to-read diagrams, the book provides excellent explanations behind the technology of performance lighting.

The Followspot Guide *Nick Mobsby* **£28.95** ISBN 9781904031499
The first in ETP's Equipment Series, Nick Mobsby's Followspot Guide tells you everything you need to know about followspots, from their history through to maintenance and usage. It's pages include a technical specification of 193 followspots from historical to the latest 2007 versions from major manufacturers.

From Ancient Rome to Rock 'n' Roll – a Review of the UK Leisure Security Industry *Mick Upton* **£14.95** ISBN 9781904031505
From stewarding, close protection and crowd management through to his engagement as a senior consultant Mick Upton has been ever present in the events industry. A founder of ShowSec International in 1982 he was its chairman until 2000. The author has led the way on training within the sector. He set up the ShowSec Training Centre and has acted as a consultant at the Bramshill Police College. He has been prominent in the development

of courses at Buckinghamshire New University where he was awarded a Doctorate in 2005. Mick has received numerous industry awards. His book is a personal account of the development and professionalism of the sector across the past 50 years.

Gobos for Image Projection *Michael Hall and Julie Harper* **£25.95**
ISBN 9781904031628
In this first published book dedicated totally to the gobo, the authors take the reader through from the history of projection to the development of the present day gobo. And there is broad practical advice and ample reference information to back it up. A feature of the work is the inclusion, interspersed throughout the text, of comment and personal experience in the use and application of gobos from over 25 leading lighting designers worldwide.

Health and Safety Aspects in the Live Music Industry *Chris Kemp, Iain Hill* **£30.00**
ISBN 1904031226
This title includes chapters on various safety aspects of live event production and is written by specialists in their particular areas of expertise.

Health and Safety Management in the Live Music and Events Industry *Chris Hannam*
£25.95 ISBN 1904031307
This title covers the health and safety regulations and their application regarding all aspects of staging live entertainment events, and is an invaluable manual for production managers and event organisers.

Hearing the Light – 50 Years Backstage *Francis Reid* **£24.95** ISBN 1904031188
This highly enjoyable memoir delves deeply into the theatricality of the industry. The author's almost fanatical interest in opera, his formative period as lighting designer at Glyndebourne and his experiences as a theatre administrator, writer and teacher make for a broad and unique background.

An Introduction to Rigging in the Entertainment Industry *Chris Higgs* **£24.95**
ISBN 1904031129
This book is a practical guide to rigging techniques and practices and also thoroughly covers safety issues and discusses the implications of working within recommended guidelines and regulations. Second edition revised September 2008.

Let There be Light – Entertainment Lighting Software Pioneers in Conversation
Robert Bell **£32.00** ISBN 1904031242
Robert Bell interviews a distinguished group of software engineers working on entertainment lighting ideas and products.

Light and Colour Filters *Michael Hall and Eddie Ruffell* **£23.95** ISBN 9781904031598
Written by two acknowledged and respected experts in the field, this book is destined to become the standard reference work on the subject. The title chronicles the development and use of colour filters and also describes how colour is perceived and how filters function. Up-to-date reference tables will help the practitioner make better and more specific choices of colour.

Lighting for Roméo and Juliette *John Offord* **£26.95** ISBN 1904031161
John Offord describes the making of the Vienna State Opera production from the lighting designer's viewpoint – from the point where director Jürgen Flimm made his decision not to use scenery or sets and simply employ the expertise of LD Patrick Woodroffe.

Lighting Systems for TV Studios *Nick Mobsby* **£45.00** ISBN 1904031005
Lighting Systems for TV Studios, now in its second edition, is the first book specifically written on the subject and has become the 'standard' resource work for studio planning and design covering the key elements of system design, luminaires, dimming, control, data networks and suspension systems as well as detailing the infrastructure items such as cyclorama, electrical and ventilation. Sensibly TV lighting principles are explained and some history on TV broadcasting, camera technology and the equipment is provided to help set the scene! The second edition includes applications for sine wave and distributed dimming, moving lights, Ethernet and new cool lamp technology.

Lighting Techniques for Theatre-in-the-Round *Jackie Staines* **£24.95** ISBN 1904031013
Lighting Techniques for Theatre-in-the-Round is a unique reference source for those working on lighting design for theatre-in-the-round for the first time. It is the first title to be published specifically on the subject, it also provides some anecdotes and ideas for more challenging shows, and attempts to blow away some of the myths surrounding lighting in this format.

Lighting the Stage *Francis Reid* **£14.95** ISBN 1904031080
Lighting the Stage discusses the human relationships involved in lighting design – both between people, and between these people and technology. The book is written from a highly personal viewpoint and its 'thinking aloud' approach is one that Francis Reid has used in his writings over the past 30 years.

Model National Standard Conditions *ABTT/DSA/LGLA* **£20.00** ISBN 1904031110
These *Model National Standard Conditions* covers operational matters and complement *The Technical Standards for Places of Entertainment,* which describes the physical requirements for building and maintaining entertainment premises.

Mr Phipps' Theatre *Mark Jones, John Pick* **£17.95** ISBN: 1904031382
Mark Jones and John Pick describe "The Sensational Story of Eastbourne's Royal Hippodrome" – formerly Eastbourne Theatre Royal. An intriguing narrative, the book sets the story against a unique social history of the town. Peter Longman, former director of The Theatres Trust, provides the Foreword.

Pages From Stages *Anthony Field* **£17.95** ISBN 1904031269
Anthony Field explores the changing style of theatres including interior design, exterior design, ticket and seat prices, and levels of service, while questioning whether the theatre still exists as a place of entertainment for regular theatre-goers.

Performing Arts Technical Training Handbook 2009/2010 *ed: John Offord* **£19.95** ISBN 9781904031604
Published in association with the ABTT (Association of British Theatre Technicians), this

important Handbook includes fully detailed and indexed entries describing courses on backstage crafts offered by over 100 universities and colleges across the UK. A completely new research project, with accompanying website, the title also includes articles with advice for those considering a career 'behind the scenes', together with contact information and descriptions of the major organisations involved with industry training – plus details of companies offering training within their own premises. The Handbook will be kept in print, with a major revision annually.

Practical Dimming *Nick Mobsby* **£22.95** ISBN 19040313447

This important and easy to read title covers the history of electrical and electronic dimming, how dimmers work, current dimmer types from around the world, planning of a dimming system, looking at new sine wave dimming technology and distributed dimming. Integration of dimming into different performance venues as well as the necessary supporting electrical systems are fully detailed. Significant levels of information are provided on the many different forms and costs of potential solutions as well as how to plan specific solutions. Architectural dimming for the likes of hotels, museums and shopping centres is included. Practical Dimming is a companion book to Practical DMX and is designed for all involved in the use, operation and design of dimming systems.

Practical DMX *Nick Mobsby* **£16.95** ISBN 1904031368

In this highly topical and important title the author details the principles of DMX, how to plan a network, how to choose equipment and cables, with data on products from around the world, and how to install DMX networks for shows and on a permanently installed basis. The easy style of the book and the helpful fault finding tips, together with a review of different DMX testing devices provide an ideal companion for all lighting technicians and system designers. An introduction to Ethernet and Canbus networks are provided as well tips on analogue networks and protocol conversion. This title has been recently updated to include a new chapter on Remote Device Management that became an international standard in Summer 2006.

Practical Guide to Health and Safety in the Entertainment Industry
Marco van Beek **£14.95** ISBN 1904031048

This book is designed to provide a practical approach to Health and Safety within the Live Entertainment and Event industry. It gives industry-pertinent examples, and seeks to break down the myths surrounding Health and Safety.

Production Management *Joe Aveline* **£17.95** ISBN 1904031102

Joe Aveline's book is an in-depth guide to the role of the Production Manager, and includes real-life practical examples and 'Aveline's Fables' – anecdotes of his experiences with real messages behind them.

Rigging for Entertainment: Regulations and Practice *Chris Higgs* **£19.95**
ISBN 1904031218

Continuing where he left off with his highly successful *An Introduction to Rigging in the Entertainment Industry*, Chris Higgs' second title covers the regulations and use of equipment in greater detail.

Rock Solid Ethernet *Wayne Howell* **£24.95** ISBN 1904031293
Although aimed specifically at specifiers, installers and users of entertainment industry systems, this book will give the reader a thorough grounding in all aspects of computer networks, whatever industry they may work in. The inclusion of historical and technical 'sidebars' make for an enjoyable as well as informative read.

Sixty Years of Light Work *Fred Bentham* **£26.95** ISBN 1904031072
This title is an autobiography of one of the great names behind the development of modern stage lighting equipment and techniques.

Sound for the Stage *Patrick Finelli* **£24.95** ISBN 1904031153
Patrick Finelli's thorough manual covering all aspects of live and recorded sound for performance is a complete training course for anyone interested in working in the field of stage sound, and is a must for any student of sound.

Stage Automation *Anton Woodward* **£12.95** ISBN 9781904031567
The purpose of this book is to explain the stage automation techniques used in modern theatre to achieve some of the spectacular visual effects seen in recent years. The book is targeted at automation operators, production managers, theatre technicians, stage engineering machinery manufacturers and theatre engineering students. Topics are covered in sufficient detail to provide an insight into the thought processes that the stage automation engineer has to consider when designing a control system to control stage machinery in a modern theatre. The author has worked on many stage automation projects and developed the award-winning Impressario stage automation system.

Stage Lighting Design in Britain: The Emergence of the Lighting Designer, 1881-1950 *Nigel Morgan* **£17.95** ISBN 190403134X
This book sets out to ascertain the main course of events and the controlling factors that determined the emergence of the theatre lighting designer in Britain, starting with the introduction of incandescent electric light to the stage, and ending at the time of the first public lighting design credits around 1950. The book explores the practitioners, equipment, installations and techniques of lighting design.

Stage Lighting for Theatre Designers *Nigel Morgan* **£17.95** ISBN 1904031196
This is an updated second edition of Nigel Morgan's popular book for students of theatre design – outlining all the techniques of stage lighting design.

Technical Marketing Techniques *David Brooks, Andy Collier, Steve Norman* **£24.95** ISBN 190403103X
Technical Marketing is a novel concept, recently defined and elaborated by the authors of this book, with business-to-business companies competing in fast developing technical product sectors.

Technical Standards for Places of Entertainment *ABTT/DSA* **£45.00** ISBN 9781904031536
Technical Standards for Places of Entertainment details the necessary physical standards required for entertainment venues. New A4 revised edition June 2008.

Theatre Engineering and Stage Machinery *Toshiro Ogawa* **£30.00**
ISBN 9781904031024
Theatre Engineering and Stage Machinery is a unique reference work covering every aspect of theatrical machinery and stage technology in global terms, and across the complete historical spectrum. Revised February 2007.

Theatre Lighting in the Age of Gas *Terence Rees* **£24.95** ISBN 190403117X
Entertainment Technology Press has republished this valuable historic work previously produced by the Society for Theatre Research in 1978. *Theatre Lighting in the Age of Gas* investigates the technological and artistic achievements of theatre lighting engineers from the 1700s to the late Victorian period.

Theatre Space: A Rediscovery Reported *Francis Reid* **£19.95** ISBN 1904031439
In the post-war world of the 1950s and 60s, the format of theatre space became a matter for a debate that aroused passions of an intensity unknown before or since. The proscenium arch was clearly identified as the enemy, accused of forming a barrier to disrupt the relations between the actor and audience. An uneasy fellow-traveller at the time, Francis Reid later recorded his impressions whilst enjoying performances or working in theatres old and new and this book is an important collection of his writings in various theatrical journals from 1969-2001 including his contribution to the Cambridge Guide to the Theatre in 1988. It reports some of the flavour of the period when theatre architecture was rediscovering its past in a search to establish its future.

Theatres of Achievement *John Higgins* **£29.95** ISBN: 1904031374
John Higgins affectionately describes the history of 40 distinguished UK theatres in a personal tribute, each uniquely illustrated by the author. Completing each profile is colour photography by Adrian Eggleston.

Theatric Tourist *Francis Reid* **£19.95** ISBN 9781904031468
Theatric Tourist is the delightful story of Francis Reid's visits across more than 50 years to theatres, theatre museums, performances and even movie theme parks. In his inimitable style, the author involves the reader within a personal experience of venues from the Legacy of Rome to theatres of the Renaissance and Eighteenth Century Baroque and the Gustavian Theatres of Stockholm. His performance experiences include Wagner in Beyreuth, the Pleasures of Tivoli and Wayang in Singapore. This is a 'must have' title for those who are as "incurably stagestruck" as the author.

Through the Viewfinder *Jeremy Hoare* **£21.95** ISBN: 9781904031574
Do you want to be a top television cameraman? Well this is going to help!
Through the Viewfinder is aimed at media students wanting to be top professional television cameramen – but it will also be of interest to anyone who wants to know what goes on behind the cameras that bring so much into our homes.
The author takes his own opinionated look at how to operate a television camera based on 23 years' experience looking through many viewfinders for a major ITV network company. Based on interviews with people he has worked with, all leaders in the profession, the book is based on their views and opinions and is a highly revealing portrait of what happens behind the scenes in television production from a cameraman's point of view.

Walt Disney Concert Hall – The Backstage Story *Patricia MacKay & Richard Pilbrow*
£28.95 ISBN 1904031234
Spanning the 16-year history of the design and construction of the Walt Disney Concert Hall, this book provides a fresh and detailed behind the scenes story of the design and technology from a variety of viewpoints. This is the first book to reveal the "process" of the design of a concert hall.

Yesterday's Lights – A Revolution Reported *Francis Reid* **£26.95** ISBN 1904031323
Set to help new generations to be aware of where the art and science of theatre lighting is coming from – and stimulate a nostalgia trip for those who lived through the period, Francis Reid's latest book has over 350 pages dedicated to the task, covering the 'revolution' from the fifties through to the present day. Although this is a highly personal account of the development of lighting design and technology and he admits that there are 'gaps', you'd be hard put to find anything of significance missing.

Go to www.etbooks.co.uk for full details of above titles and secure online ordering facilities.